KNIGHTS OF YORK

KNIGHTS OF YORK

JIMMY PALMIOTTI & JUSTIN GRAY

ADAPTIVE
COMICS   PAPERFILMS

WRITTEN BY: **JIMMY PALMIOTTI & JUSTIN GRAY**

ART BY: **STAZ JOHNSON**

INKS BY: **STAZ JOHNSON AND MARIA KEANE**

COLORING AND LETTERING: **CHALLENGING STUDIOS**

COVER: **COLD OPEN**

DESIGN BY: **TORNADO CREATIVE**

CO-PUBLISHED BY **PAPERFILMS & ADAPTIVE STUDIOS**

KNIGHTS OF YORK First Exclusive Printing. November 2017. Co-published by PaperFilms &
Adaptive Comics. Clearwater, Florida 33759. Copyright © 2017 PaperFilms, Inc. & Adaptive Studios.
All rights reserved.

KNIGHTS OF YORK (including all prominent characters featured herein) are trademarks of PaperFilms,
Inc. & Adaptive Studios, unless otherwise noted. No part of this publication may be reproduced or
transmitted, in any form or by any means (except for short excerpts for review purposes) without
the express written permission of PaperFilms. All names, characters, events and locales in this
publication are entirely fictional. Any resemblance to actual persons (living or dead), events or places,
without satiric intent, is coincidental.

VISIT US ON THE WEB AT **WWW.ADAPTIVESTUDIOS.COM**

Library of Congress Cataloging in Publication Number: 2017949894
B&N ISBN: 978-1-945293-39-9
ISBN: 978-1-945293-57-3
Ebook ISBN: 978-1-945293-55-9

Manufactured in China.

Adaptive Comics
3578 Hayden Avenue, Suite 6
Culver City, CA 90232

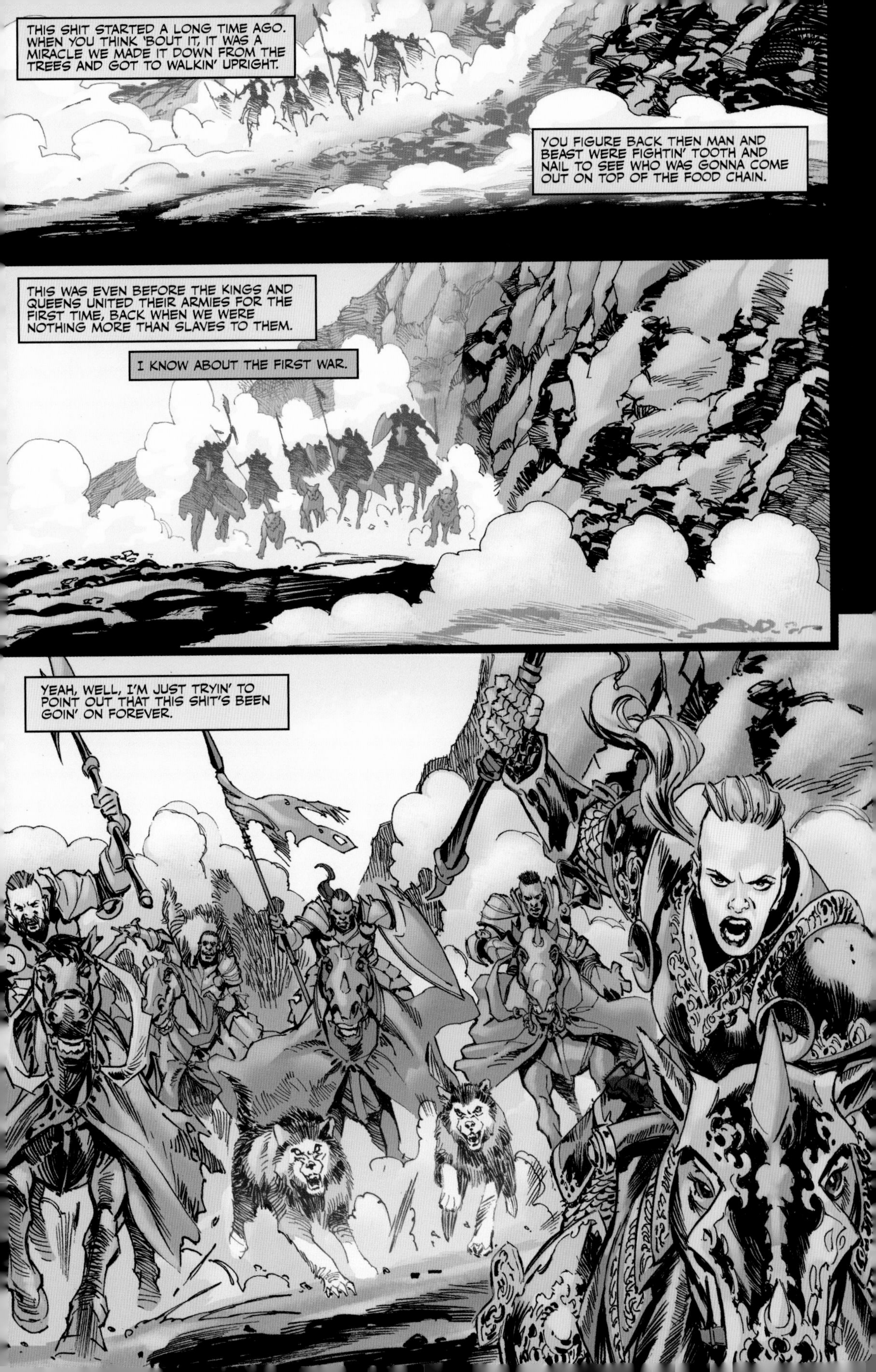
THIS SHIT STARTED A LONG TIME AGO. WHEN YOU THINK 'BOUT IT, IT WAS A MIRACLE WE MADE IT DOWN FROM THE TREES AND GOT TO WALKIN' UPRIGHT.
YOU FIGURE BACK THEN MAN AND BEAST WERE FIGHTIN' TOOTH AND NAIL TO SEE WHO WAS GONNA COME OUT ON TOP OF THE FOOD CHAIN.
THIS WAS EVEN BEFORE THE KINGS AND QUEENS UNITED THEIR ARMIES FOR THE FIRST TIME, BACK WHEN WE WERE NOTHING MORE THAN SLAVES TO THEM.
I KNOW ABOUT THE FIRST WAR.
YEAH, WELL, I'M JUST TRYIN' TO POINT OUT THAT THIS SHIT'S BEEN GOIN' ON FOREVER.

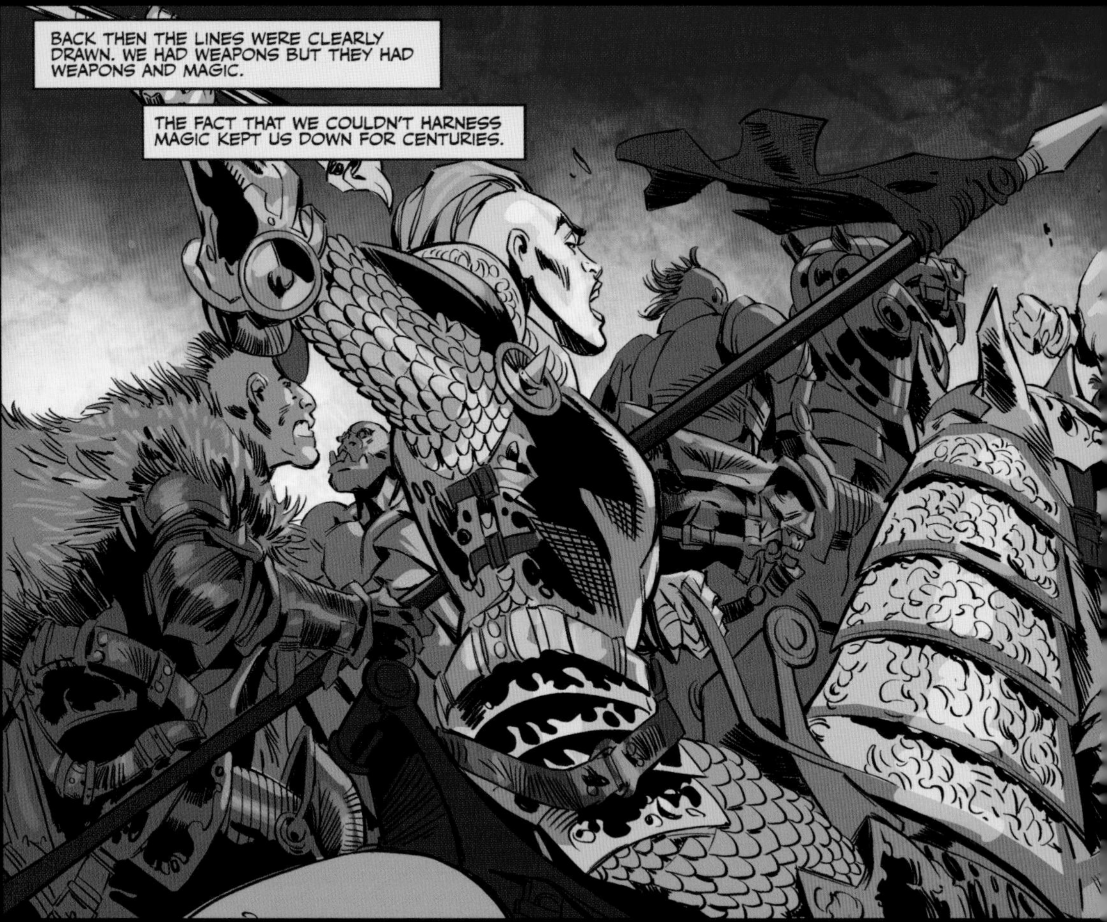
BACK THEN THE LINES WERE CLEARLY DRAWN. WE HAD WEAPONS BUT THEY HAD WEAPONS AND MAGIC.
THE FACT THAT WE COULDN'T HARNESS MAGIC KEPT US DOWN FOR CENTURIES.

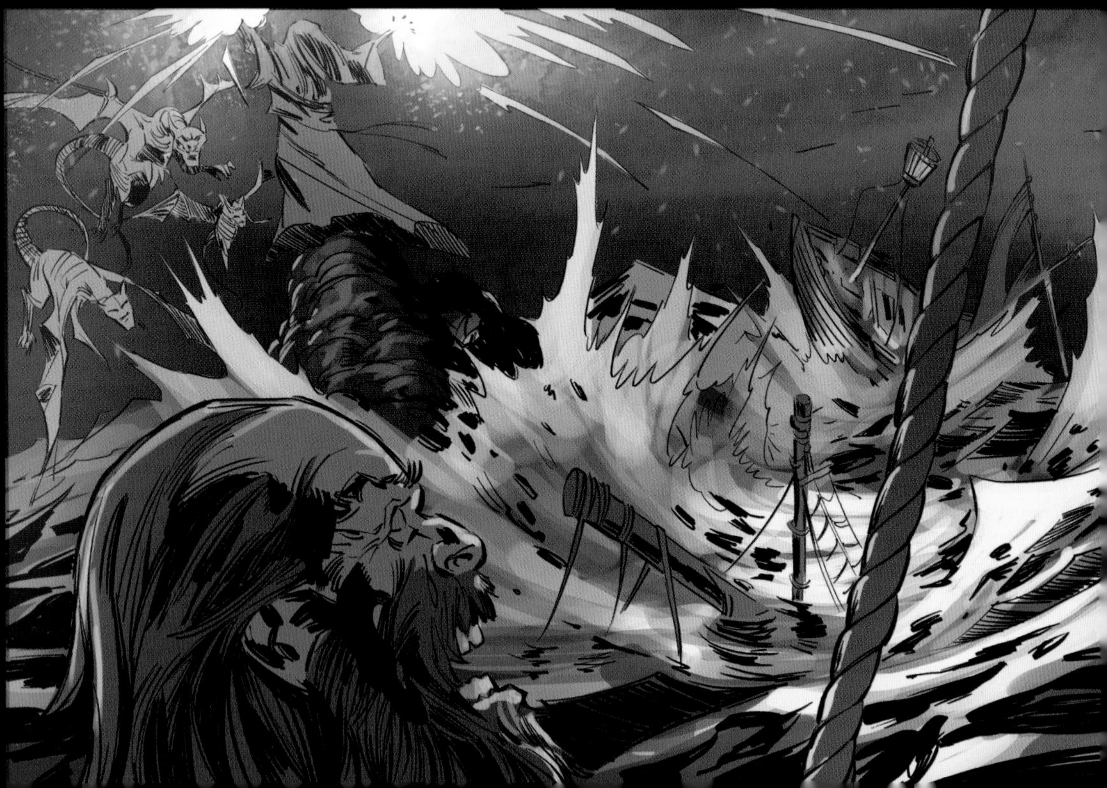

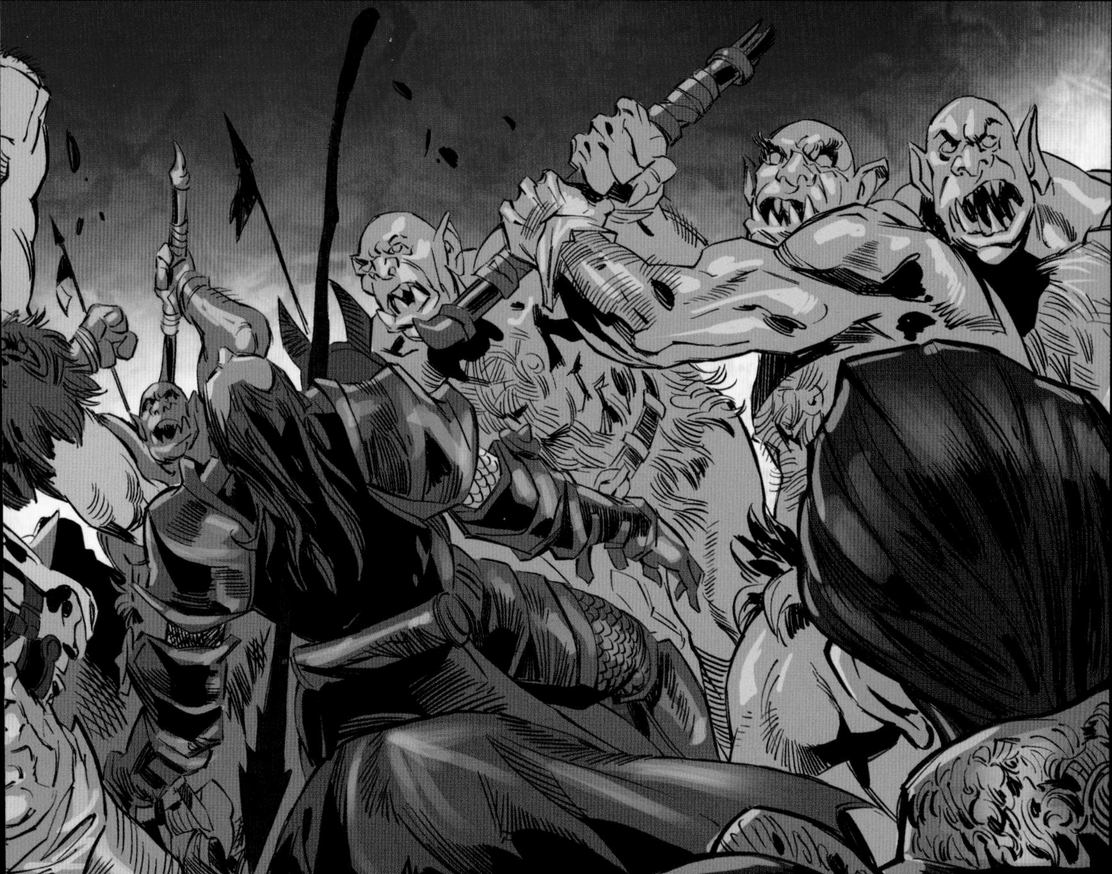

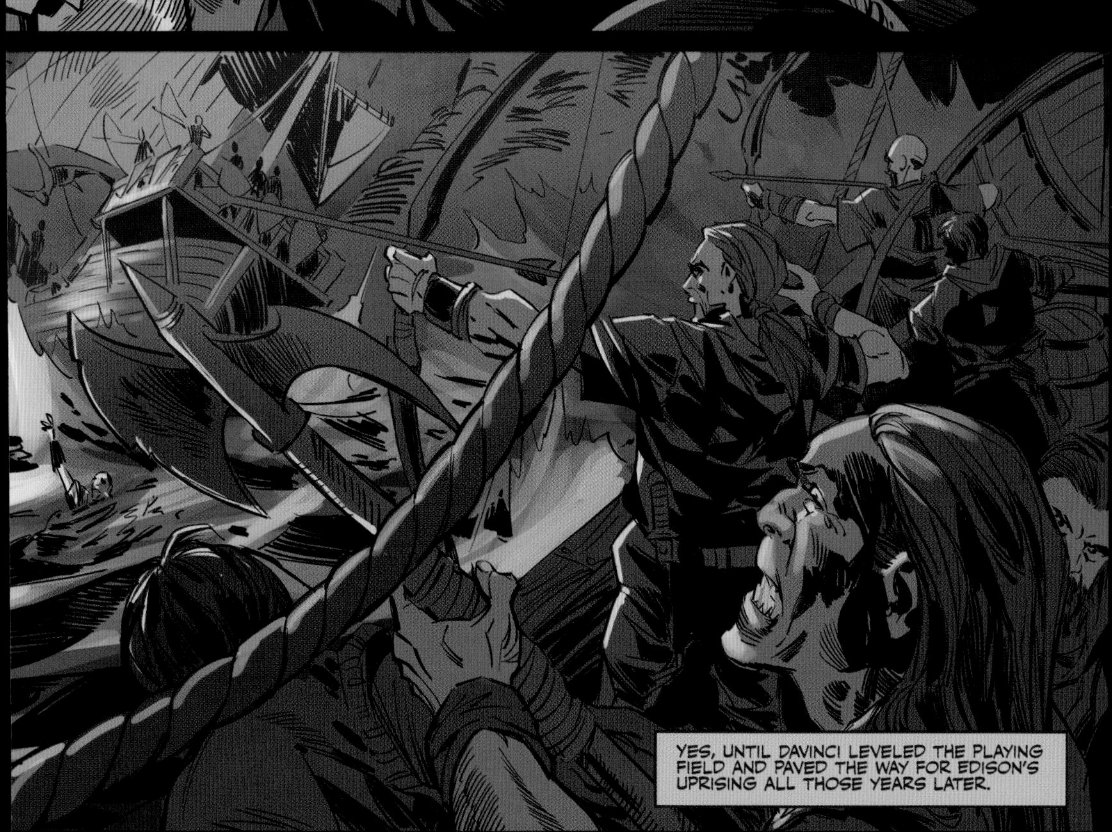
YES, UNTIL DAVINCI LEVELED THE PLAYING FIELD AND PAVED THE WAY FOR EDISON'S UPRISING ALL THOSE YEARS LATER.

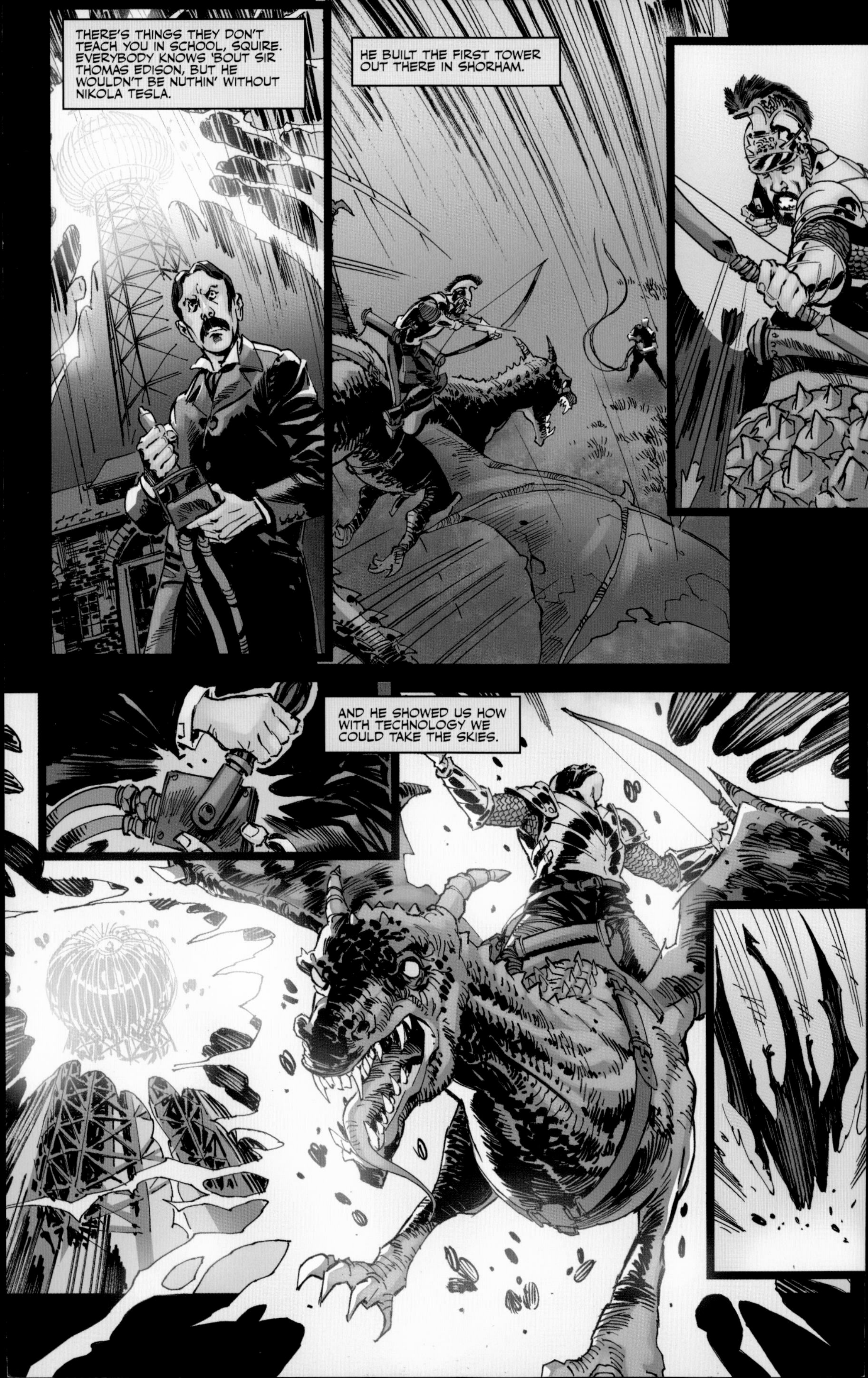
THERE'S THINGS THEY DON'T TEACH YOU IN SCHOOL, SQUIRE. EVERYBODY KNOWS 'BOUT SIR THOMAS EDISON, BUT HE WOULDN'T BE NUTHIN' WITHOUT NIKOLA TESLA.
HE BUILT THE FIRST TOWER OUT THERE IN SHORHAM.
AND HE SHOWED US HOW WITH TECHNOLOGY WE COULD TAKE THE SKIES.

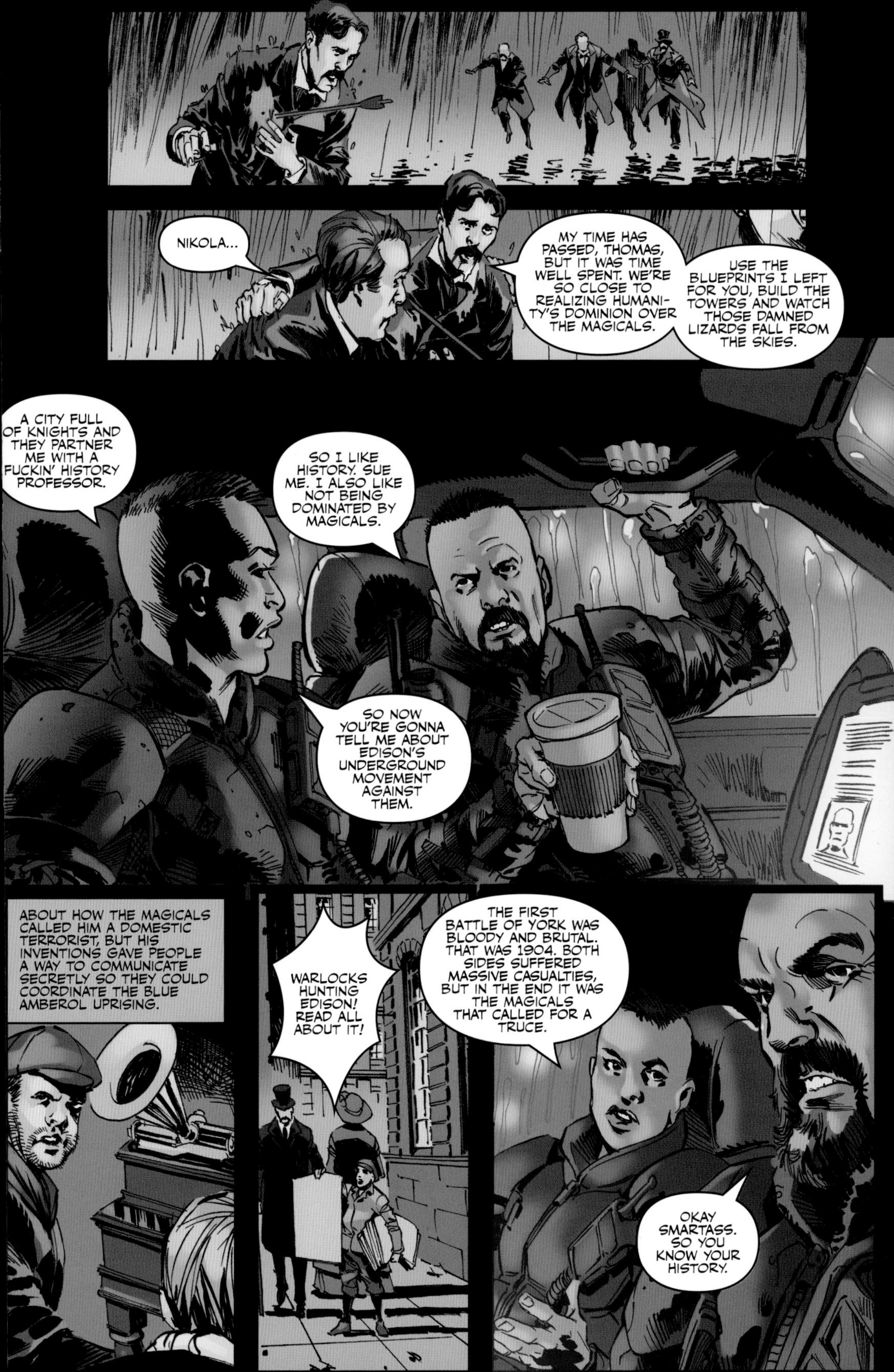
NIKOLA...
MY TIME HAS PASSED, THOMAS, BUT IT WAS TIME WELL SPENT. WE'RE SO CLOSE TO REALIZING HUMANITY'S DOMINION OVER THE MAGICALS.
USE THE BLUEPRINTS I LEFT FOR YOU, BUILD THE TOWERS AND WATCH THOSE DAMNED LIZARDS FALL FROM THE SKIES.
A CITY FULL OF KNIGHTS AND THEY PARTNER ME WITH A FUCKIN' HISTORY PROFESSOR.
SO I LIKE HISTORY. SUE ME. I ALSO LIKE NOT BEING DOMINATED BY MAGICALS.
SO NOW YOU'RE GONNA TELL ME ABOUT EDISON'S UNDERGROUND MOVEMENT AGAINST THEM.
ABOUT HOW THE MAGICALS CALLED HIM A DOMESTIC TERRORIST, BUT HIS INVENTIONS GAVE PEOPLE A WAY TO COMMUNICATE SECRETLY SO THEY COULD COORDINATE THE BLUE AMBEROL UPRISING.
WARLOCKS HUNTING EDISON! READ ALL ABOUT IT!
THE FIRST BATTLE OF YORK WAS BLOODY AND BRUTAL. THAT WAS 1904. BOTH SIDES SUFFERED MASSIVE CASUALTIES, BUT IN THE END IT WAS THE MAGICALS THAT CALLED FOR A TRUCE.
OKAY SMARTASS. SO YOU KNOW YOUR HISTORY.

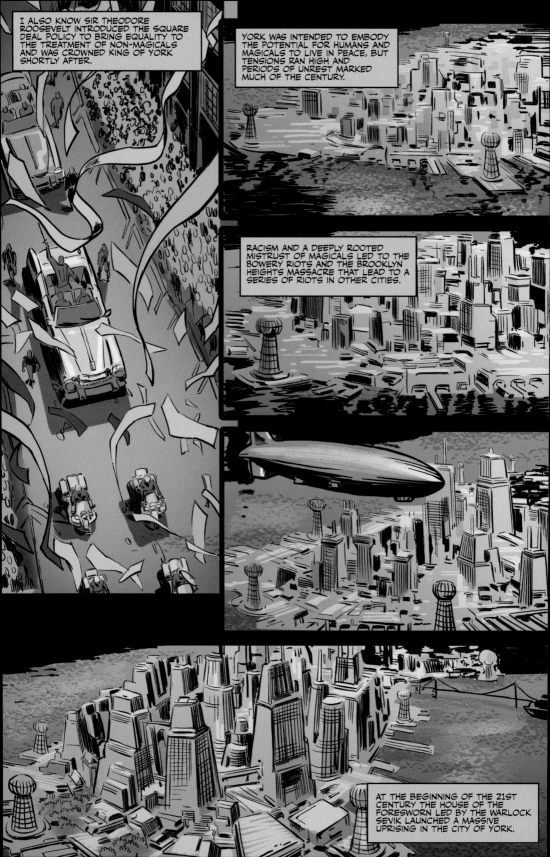

I ALSO KNOW SIR THEODORE ROOSEVELT INTRODUCED THE SQUARE DEAL POLICY TO BRING EQUALITY TO THE TREATMENT OF NON-MAGICALS AND WAS CROWNED KING OF YORK SHORTLY AFTER.

YORK WAS INTENDED TO EMBODY THE POTENTIAL FOR HUMANS AND MAGICALS TO LIVE IN PEACE, BUT TENSIONS RAN HIGH AND PERIODS OF UNREST MARKED MUCH OF THE CENTURY.

RACISM AND A DEEPLY ROOTED MISTRUST OF MAGICALS LED TO THE BOWERY RIOTS AND THE BROOKLYN HEIGHTS MASSACRE THAT LEAD TO A SERIES OF RIOTS IN OTHER CITIES.

AT THE BEGINNING OF THE 21ST CENTURY THE HOUSE OF THE FORESWORN LED BY THE WARLOCK SEVIK LAUNCHED A MASSIVE UPRISING IN THE CITY OF YORK.

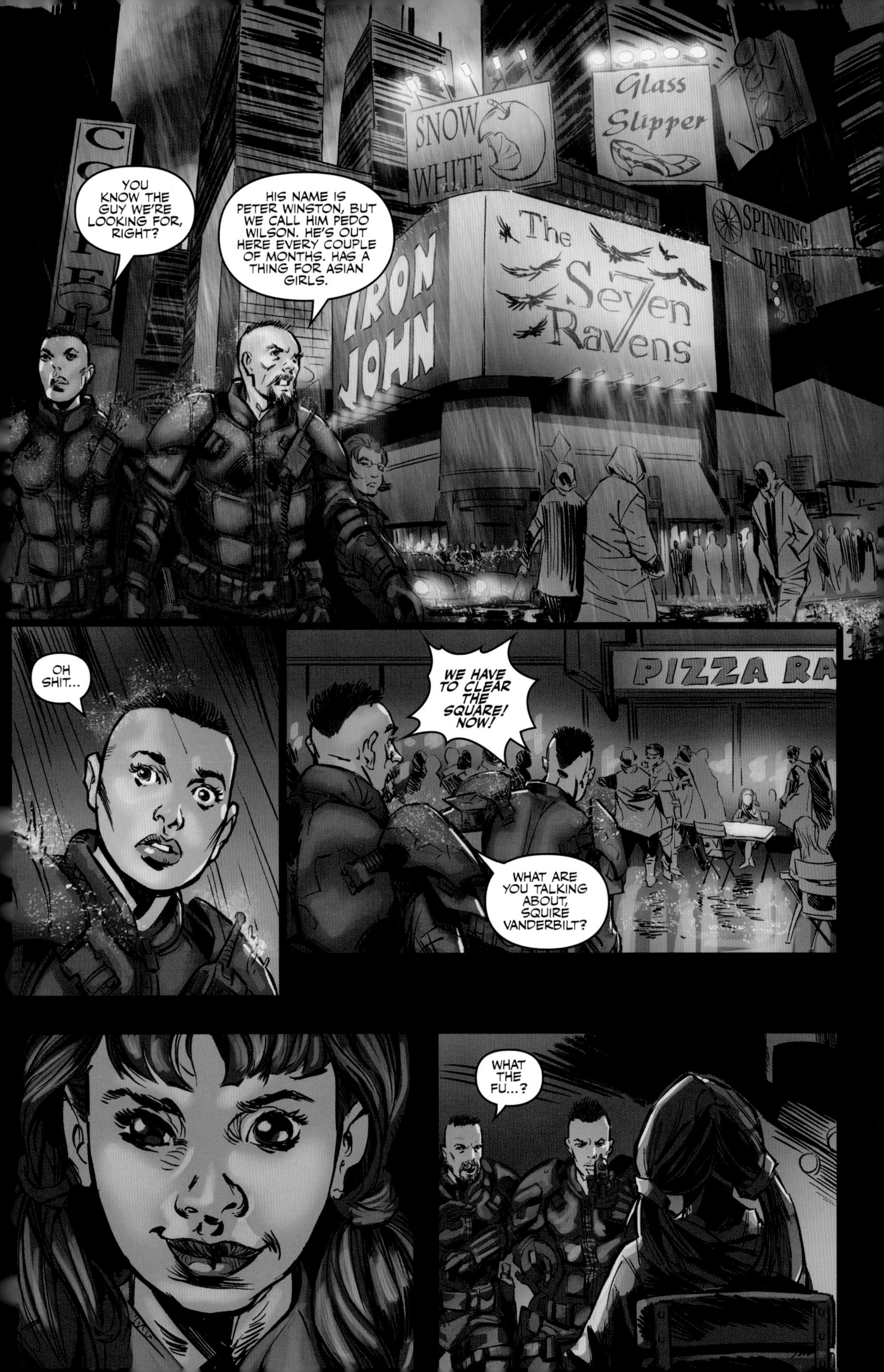
Glass Slipper
SNOW WHITE
YOU KNOW THE GUY WE'RE LOOKING FOR, RIGHT?
HIS NAME IS PETER WINSTON, BUT WE CALL HIM PEDO WILSON. HE'S OUT HERE EVERY COUPLE OF MONTHS. HAS A THING FOR ASIAN GIRLS.
IRON JOHN
The Se7en Ravens
SPINNING
OH SHIT...
WE HAVE TO CLEAR THE SQUARE! NOW!
WHAT ARE YOU TALKING ABOUT, SQUIRE VANDERBILT?
WHAT THE FU...?

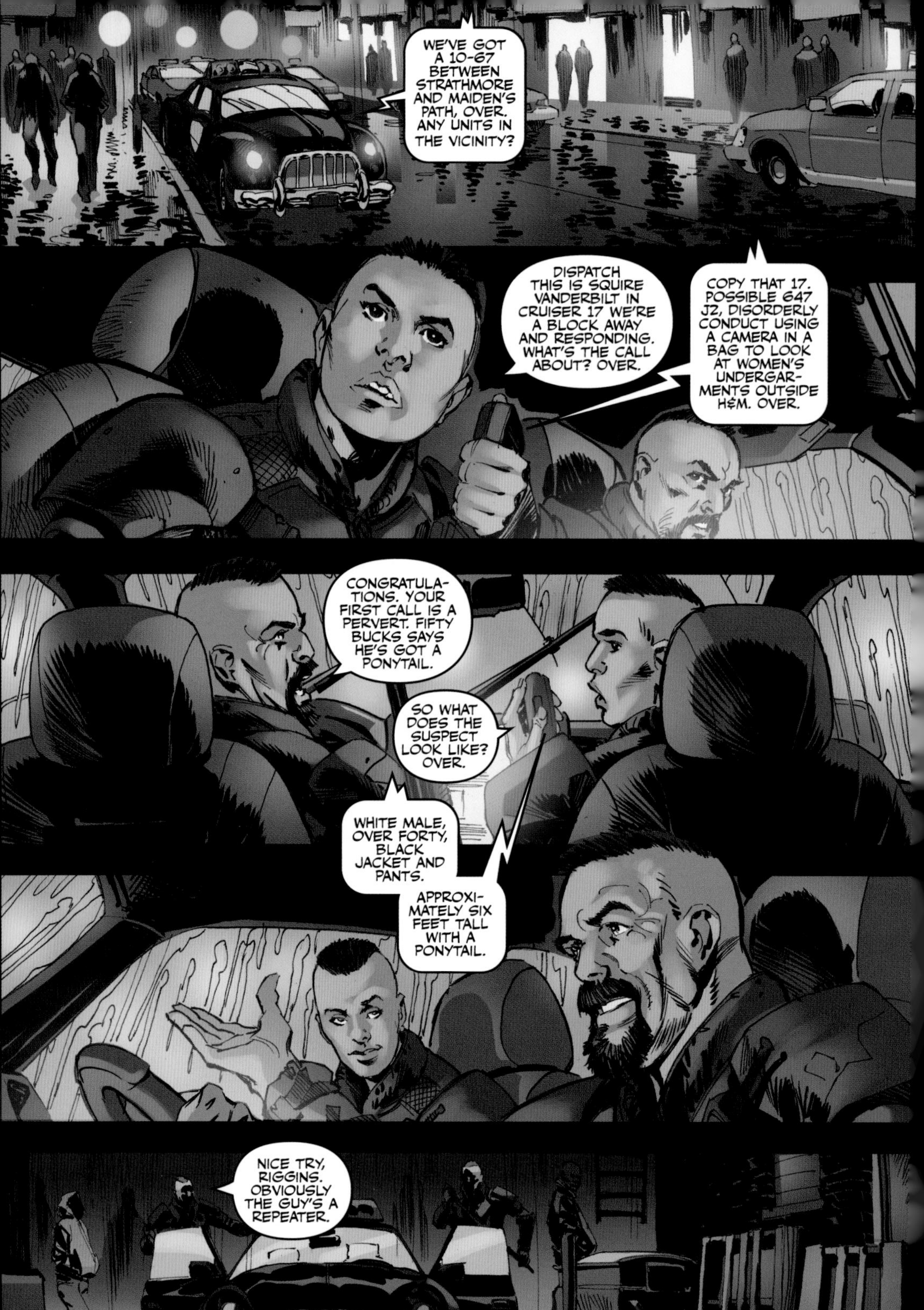
WE'VE GOT A 10-67 BETWEEN STRATHMORE AND MAIDEN'S PATH, OVER. ANY UNITS IN THE VICINITY?
DISPATCH THIS IS SQUIRE VANDERBILT IN CRUISER 17 WE'RE A BLOCK AWAY AND RESPONDING. WHAT'S THE CALL ABOUT? OVER.
COPY THAT 17. POSSIBLE 647 J2, DISORDERLY CONDUCT USING A CAMERA IN A BAG TO LOOK AT WOMEN'S UNDERGAR-MENTS OUTSIDE H&M. OVER.
CONGRATULA-TIONS. YOUR FIRST CALL IS A PERVERT. FIFTY BUCKS SAYS HE'S GOT A PONYTAIL.
SO WHAT DOES THE SUSPECT LOOK LIKE? OVER.
WHITE MALE, OVER FORTY, BLACK JACKET AND PANTS.
APPROXI-MATELY SIX FEET TALL WITH A PONYTAIL.
NICE TRY, RIGGINS. OBVIOUSLY THE GUY'S A REPEATER.

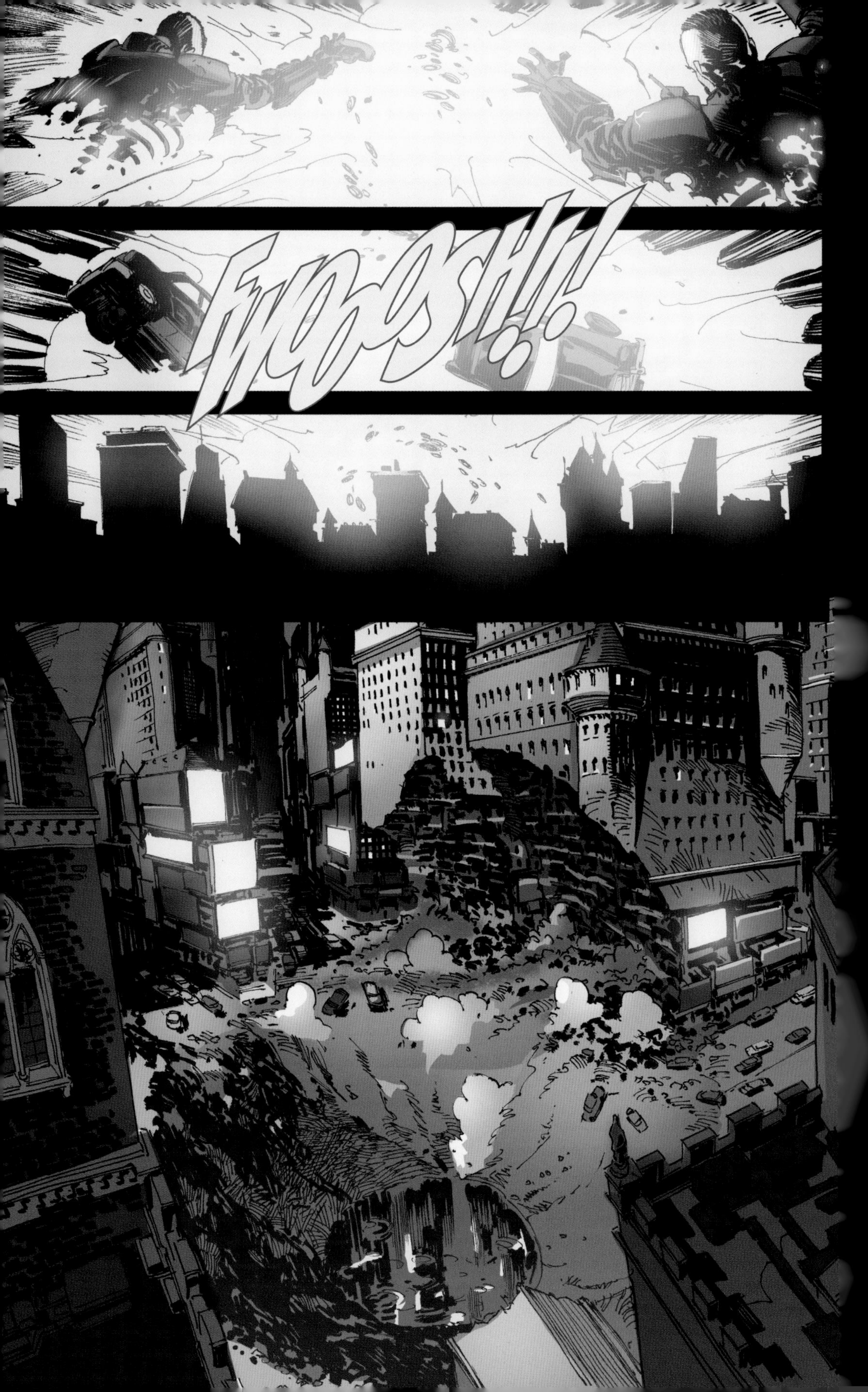
FWOOOSH!!

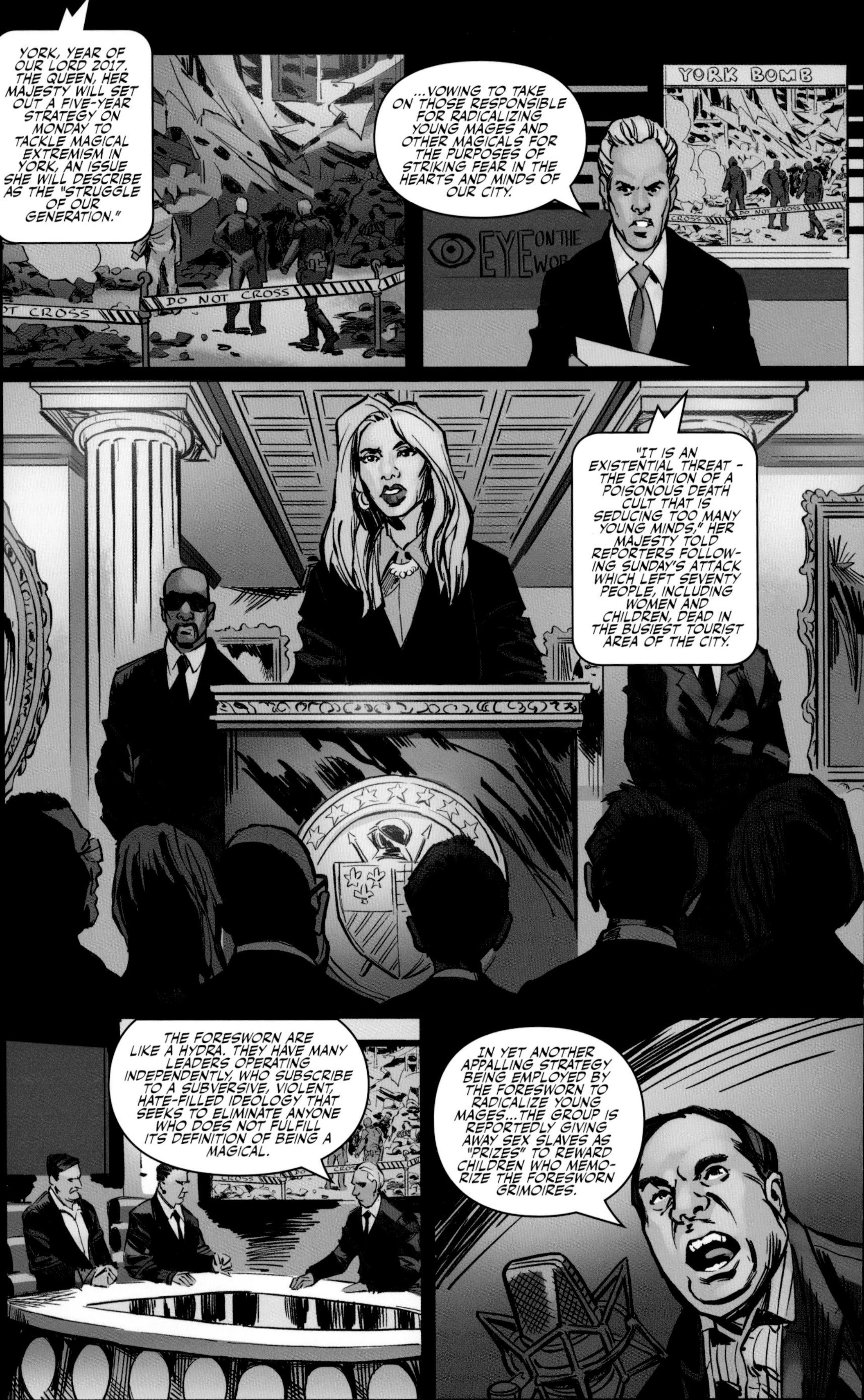
YORK, YEAR OF OUR LORD 2017. THE QUEEN, HER MAJESTY WILL SET OUT A FIVE-YEAR STRATEGY ON MONDAY TO TACKLE MAGICAL EXTREMISM IN YORK, AN ISSUE SHE WILL DESCRIBE AS THE "STRUGGLE OF OUR GENERATION."
DO NOT CROSS
...VOWING TO TAKE ON THOSE RESPONSIBLE FOR RADICALIZING YOUNG MAGES AND OTHER MAGICALS FOR THE PURPOSES OF STRIKING FEAR IN THE HEARTS AND MINDS OF OUR CITY.
YORK BOMB
EYE ON THE
"IT IS AN EXISTENTIAL THREAT - THE CREATION OF A POISONOUS DEATH CULT THAT IS SEDUCING TOO MANY YOUNG MINDS," HER MAJESTY TOLD REPORTERS FOLLOWING SUNDAY'S ATTACK WHICH LEFT SEVENTY PEOPLE, INCLUDING WOMEN AND CHILDREN, DEAD IN THE BUSIEST TOURIST AREA OF THE CITY.
THE FORESWORN ARE LIKE A HYDRA. THEY HAVE MANY LEADERS OPERATING INDEPENDENTLY, WHO SUBSCRIBE TO A SUBVERSIVE, VIOLENT, HATE-FILLED IDEOLOGY THAT SEEKS TO ELIMINATE ANYONE WHO DOES NOT FULFILL ITS DEFINITION OF BEING A MAGICAL.
IN YET ANOTHER APPALLING STRATEGY BEING EMPLOYED BY THE FORESWORN TO RADICALIZE YOUNG MAGES...THE GROUP IS REPORTEDLY GIVING AWAY SEX SLAVES AS "PRIZES" TO REWARD CHILDREN WHO MEMORIZE THE FORESWORN GRIMOIRES.

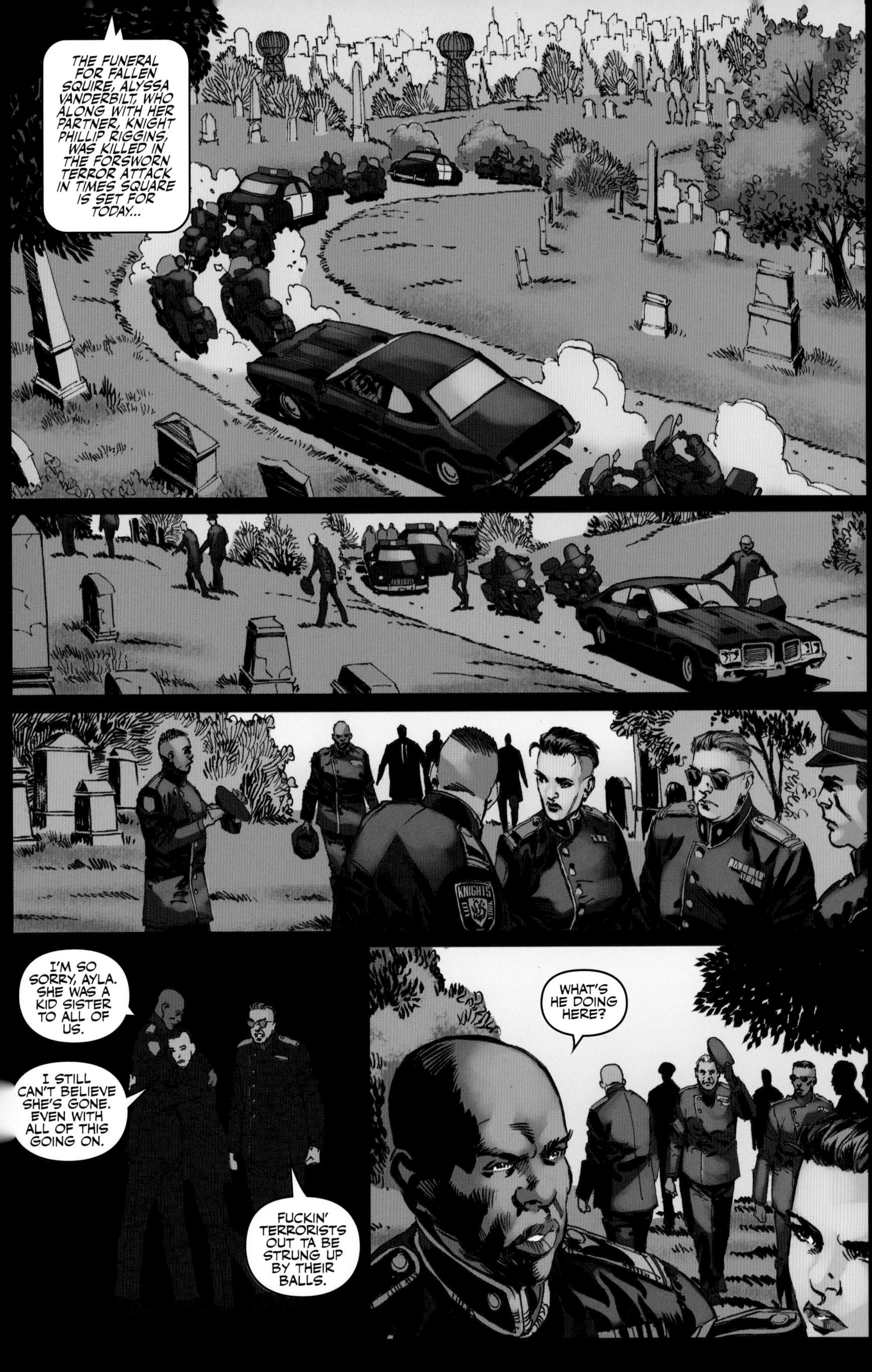
THE FUNERAL FOR FALLEN SQUIRE, ALYSSA VANDERBILT, WHO ALONG WITH HER PARTNER, KNIGHT PHILLIP RIGGINS, WAS KILLED IN THE FORSWORN TERROR ATTACK IN TIMES SQUARE IS SET FOR TODAY...
KNIGHTS CITY YORK
I'M SO SORRY, AYLA. SHE WAS A KID SISTER TO ALL OF US.
I STILL CAN'T BELIEVE SHE'S GONE. EVEN WITH ALL OF THIS GOING ON.
FUCKIN' TERRORISTS OUT TA BE STRUNG UP BY THEIR BALLS.
WHAT'S HE DOING HERE?

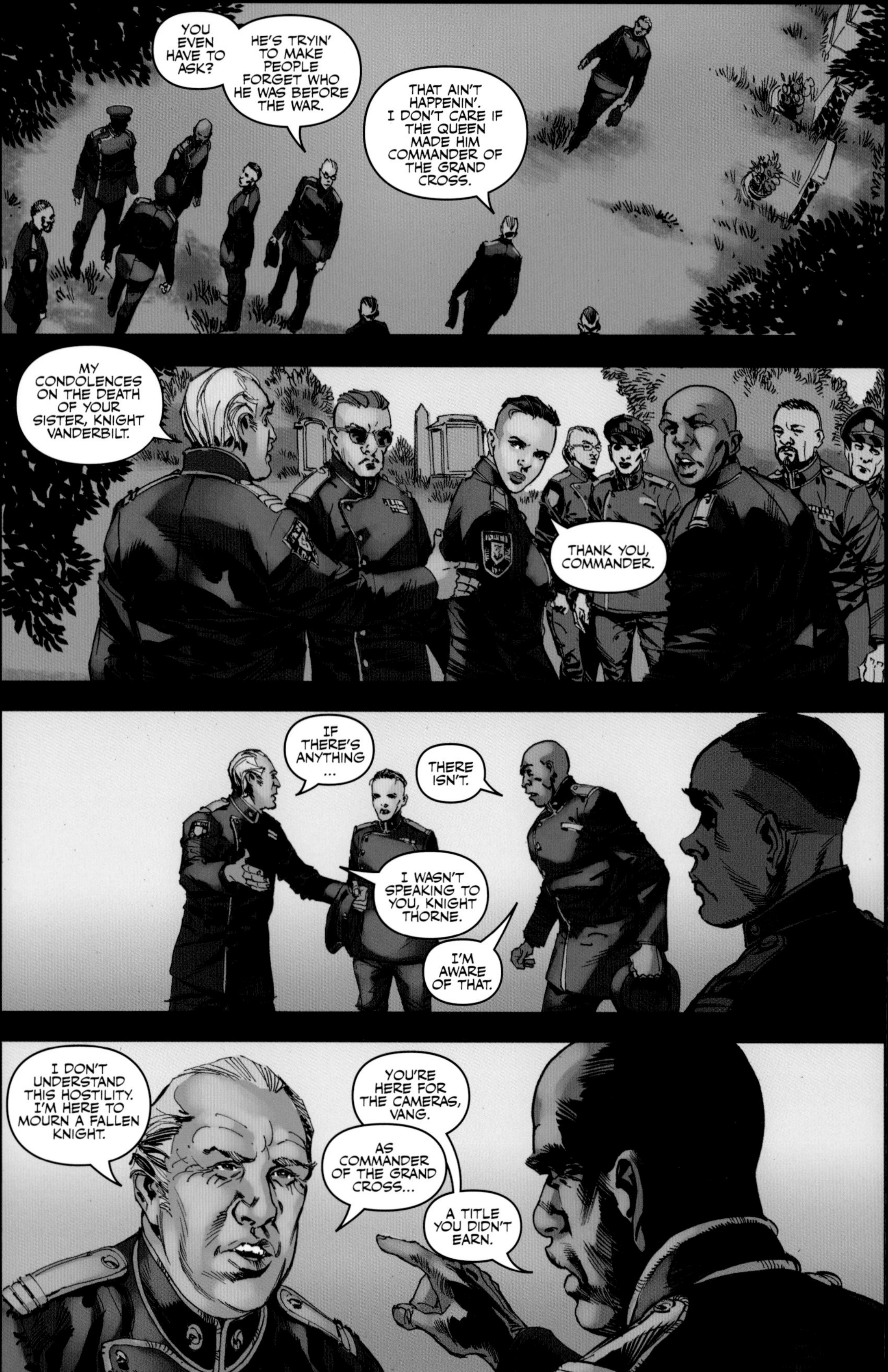
YOU EVEN HAVE TO ASK?
HE'S TRYIN' TO MAKE PEOPLE FORGET WHO HE WAS BEFORE THE WAR.
THAT AIN'T HAPPENIN'. I DON'T CARE IF THE QUEEN MADE HIM COMMANDER OF THE GRAND CROSS.
MY CONDOLENCES ON THE DEATH OF YOUR SISTER, KNIGHT VANDERBILT.
THANK YOU, COMMANDER.
IF THERE'S ANYTHING ...
THERE ISN'T.
I WASN'T SPEAKING TO YOU, KNIGHT THORNE.
I'M AWARE OF THAT.
I DON'T UNDERSTAND THIS HOSTILITY. I'M HERE TO MOURN A FALLEN KNIGHT.
YOU'RE HERE FOR THE CAMERAS, VANG.
AS COMMANDER OF THE GRAND CROSS...
A TITLE YOU DIDN'T EARN.

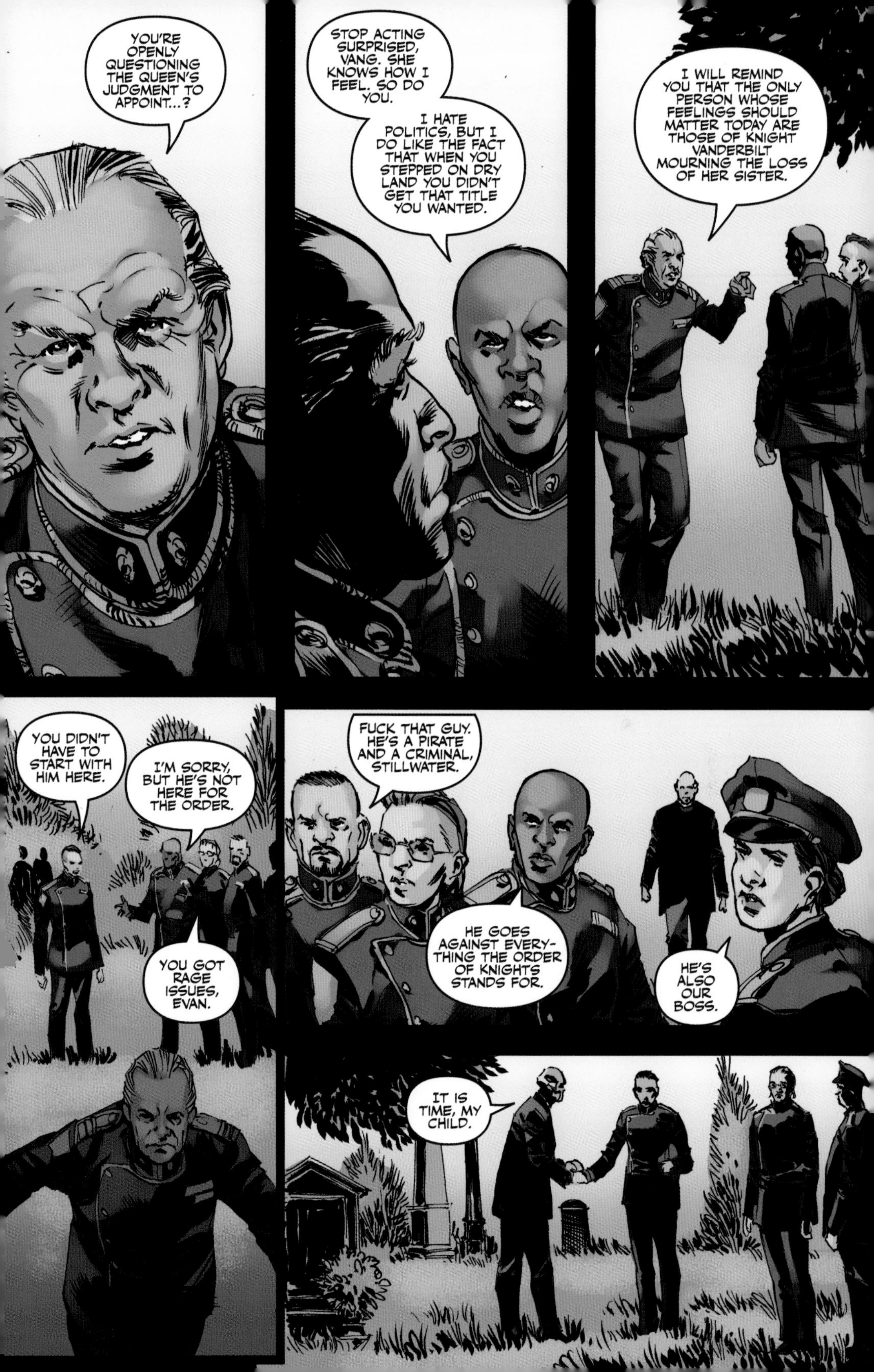
YOU'RE OPENLY QUESTIONING THE QUEEN'S JUDGMENT TO APPOINT...?
STOP ACTING SURPRISED, VANG. SHE KNOWS HOW I FEEL. SO DO YOU.
I HATE POLITICS, BUT I DO LIKE THE FACT THAT WHEN YOU STEPPED ON DRY LAND YOU DIDN'T GET THAT TITLE YOU WANTED.
I WILL REMIND YOU THAT THE ONLY PERSON WHOSE FEELINGS SHOULD MATTER TODAY ARE THOSE OF KNIGHT VANDERBILT MOURNING THE LOSS OF HER SISTER.
YOU DIDN'T HAVE TO START WITH HIM HERE.
I'M SORRY, BUT HE'S NOT HERE FOR THE ORDER.
YOU GOT RAGE ISSUES, EVAN.
FUCK THAT GUY. HE'S A PIRATE AND A CRIMINAL, STILLWATER.
HE GOES AGAINST EVERY-THING THE ORDER OF KNIGHTS STANDS FOR.
HE'S ALSO OUR BOSS.
IT IS TIME, MY CHILD.

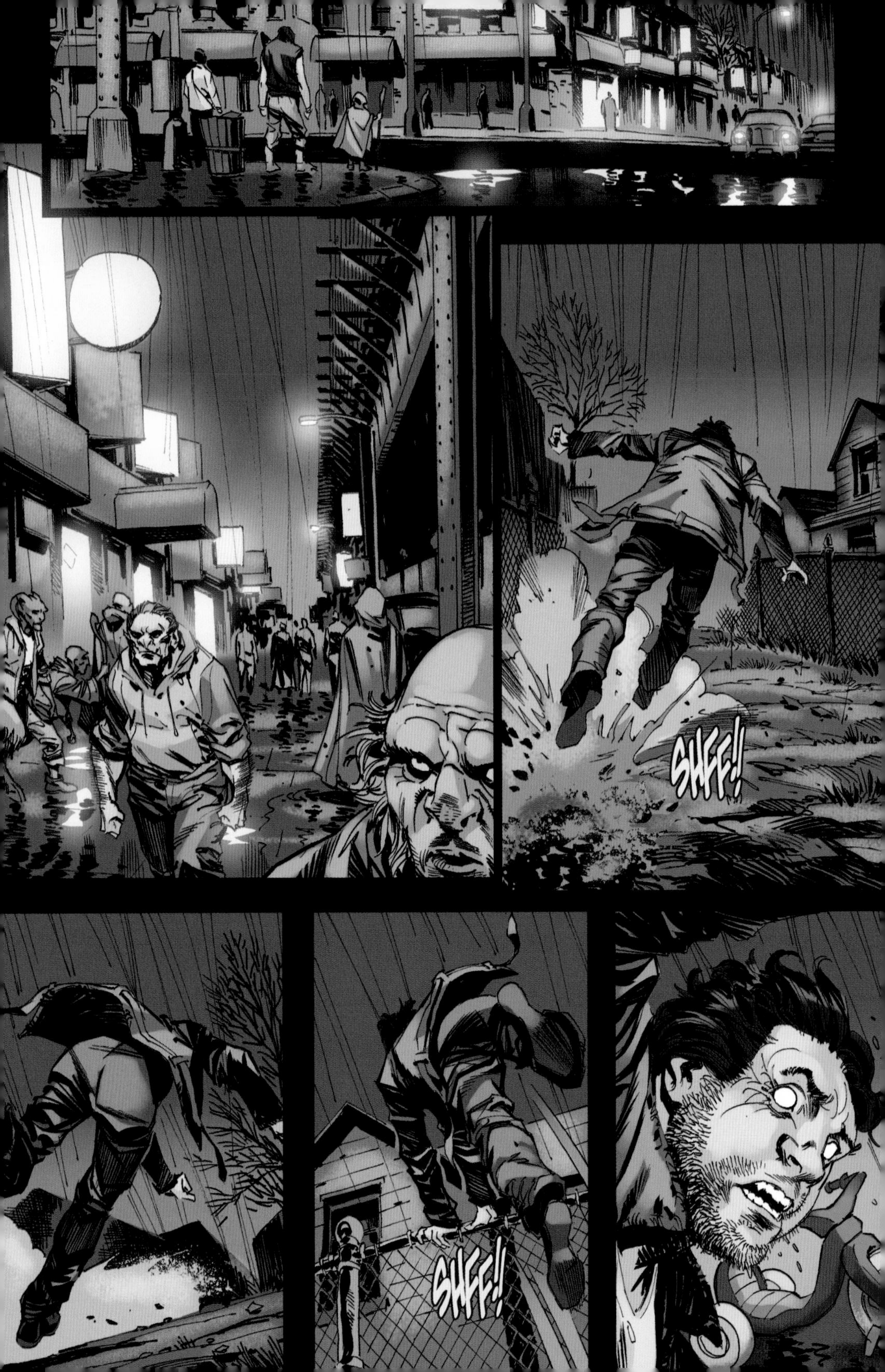
SHFF!!
SHFF!!

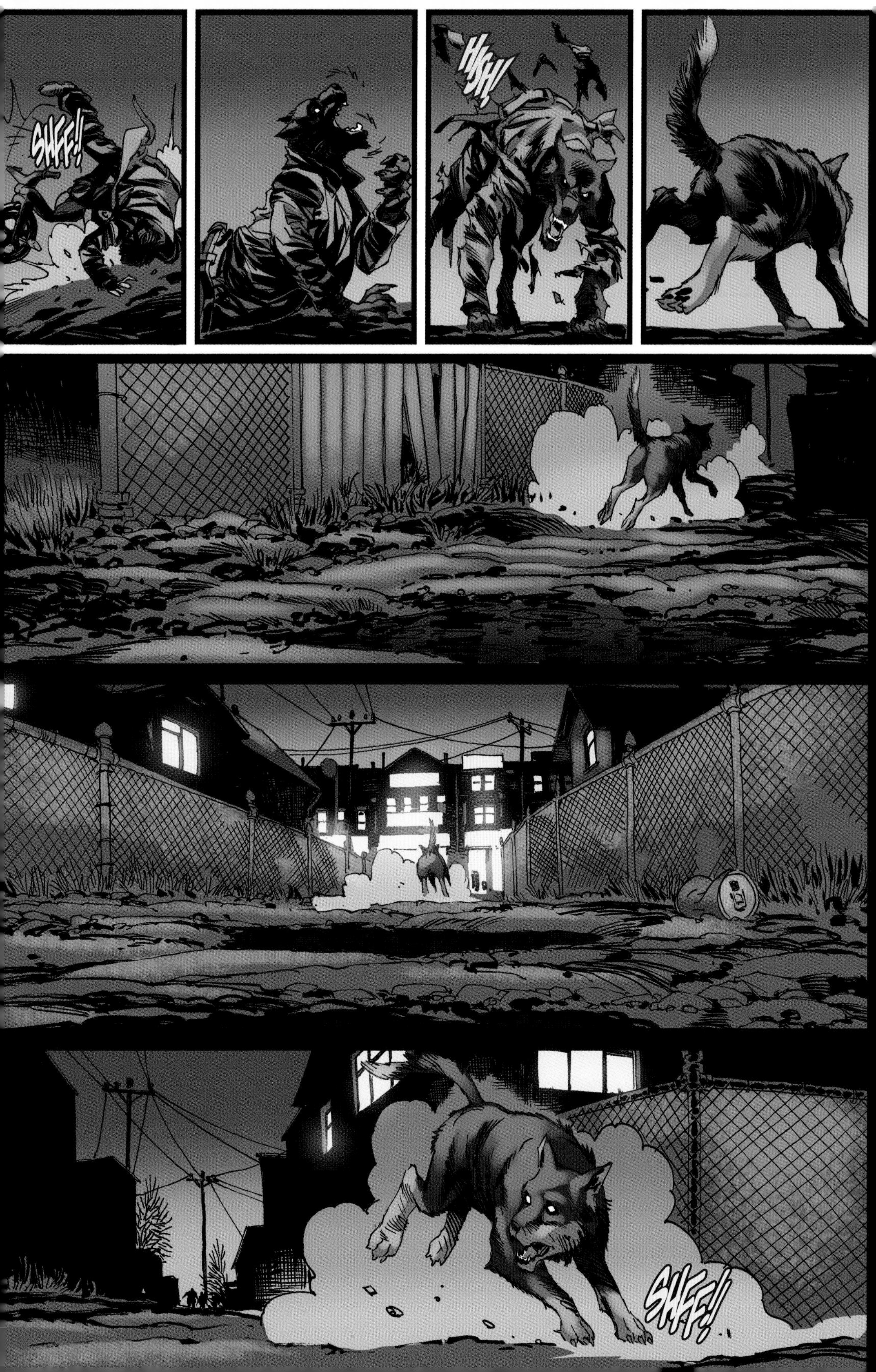
SHFF!!
HISH!
SHFF!!

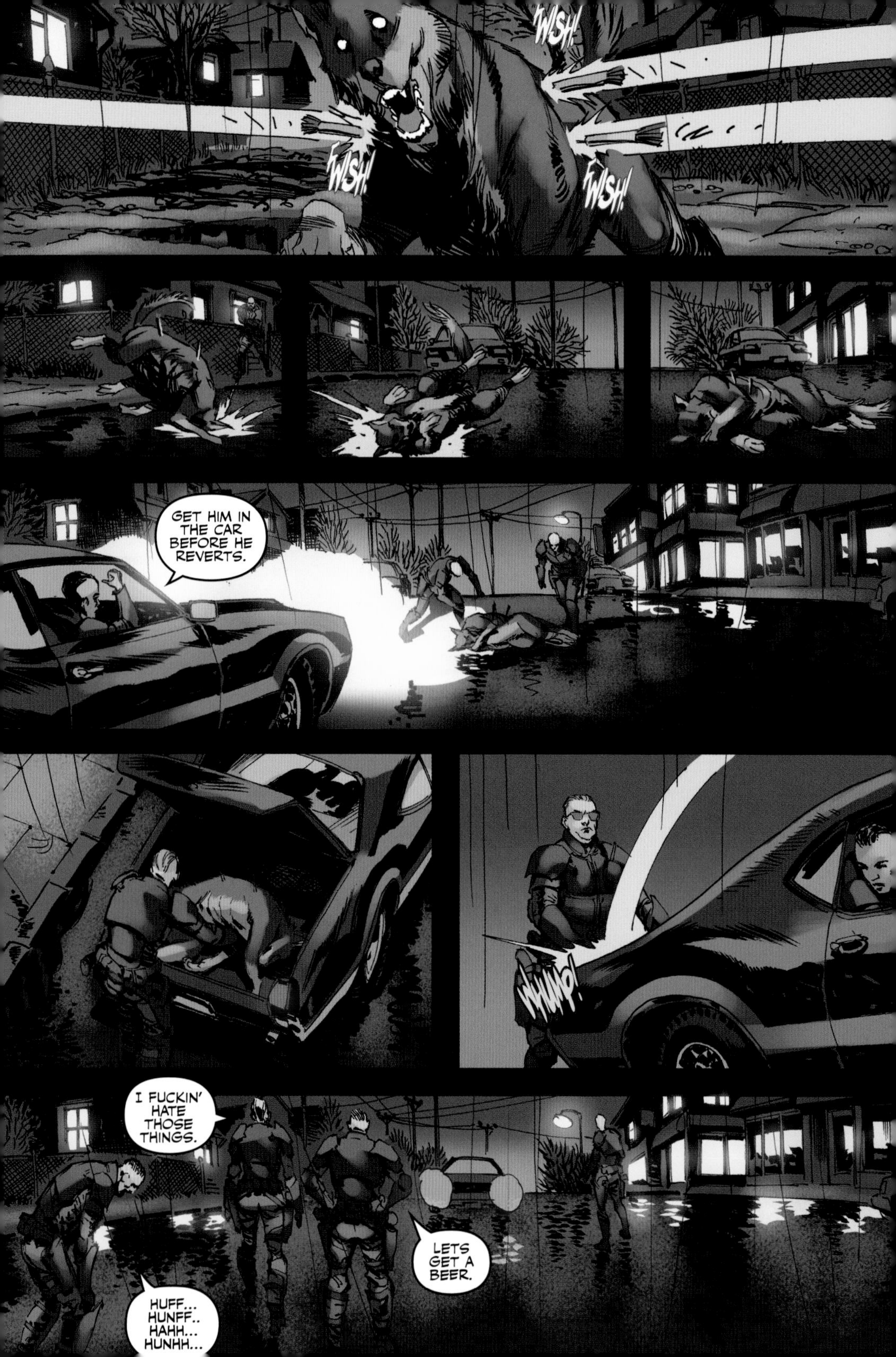
FWISH!
FWISH!
FWISH!
GET HIM IN THE CAR BEFORE HE REVERTS.
WHUMP!
I FUCKIN' HATE THOSE THINGS.
LETS GET A BEER.
HUFF... HUNFF.. HAHH... HUNHH...

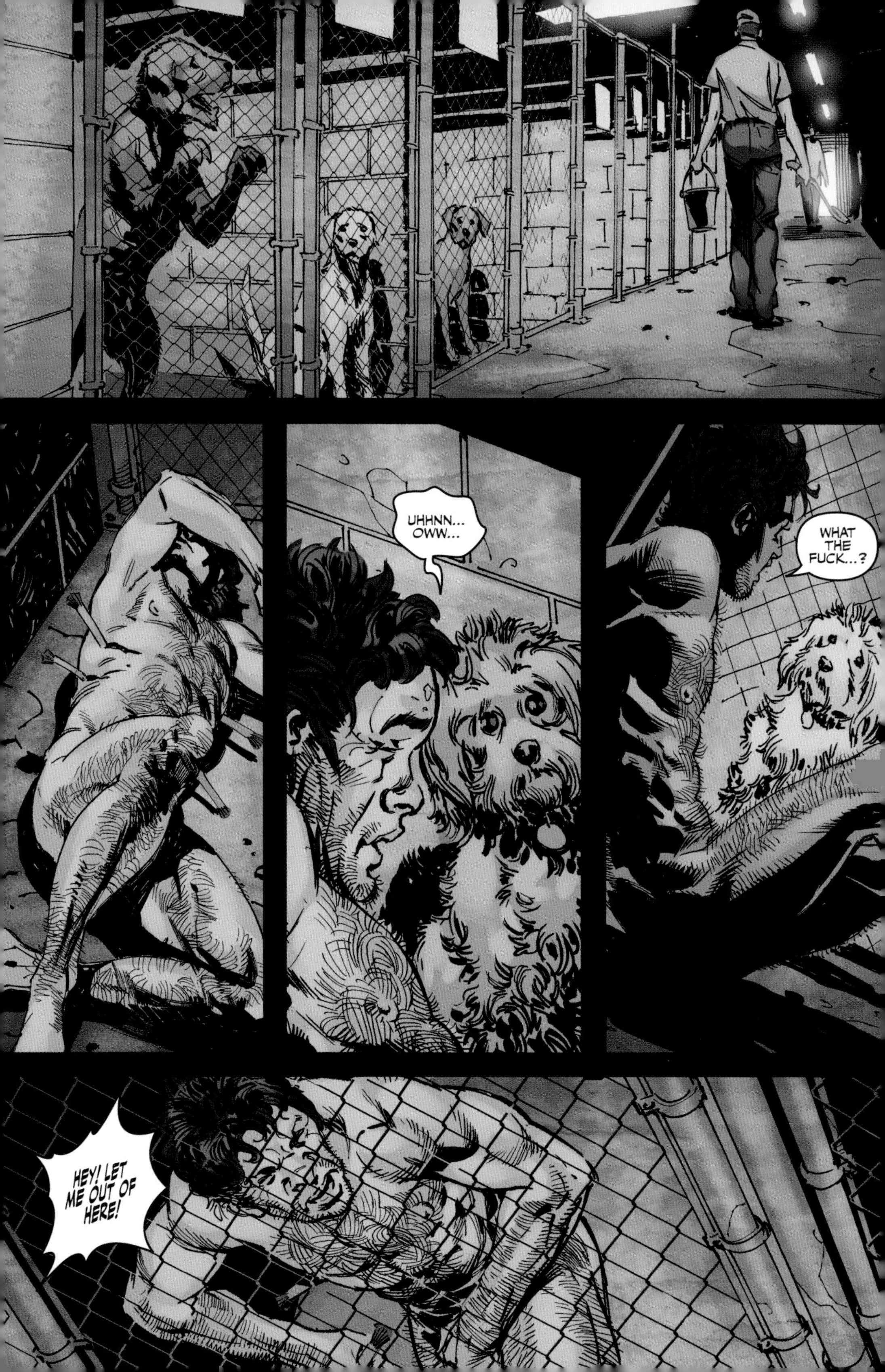
UHHNN... OWW...
WHAT THE FUCK...?
HEY! LET ME OUT OF HERE!

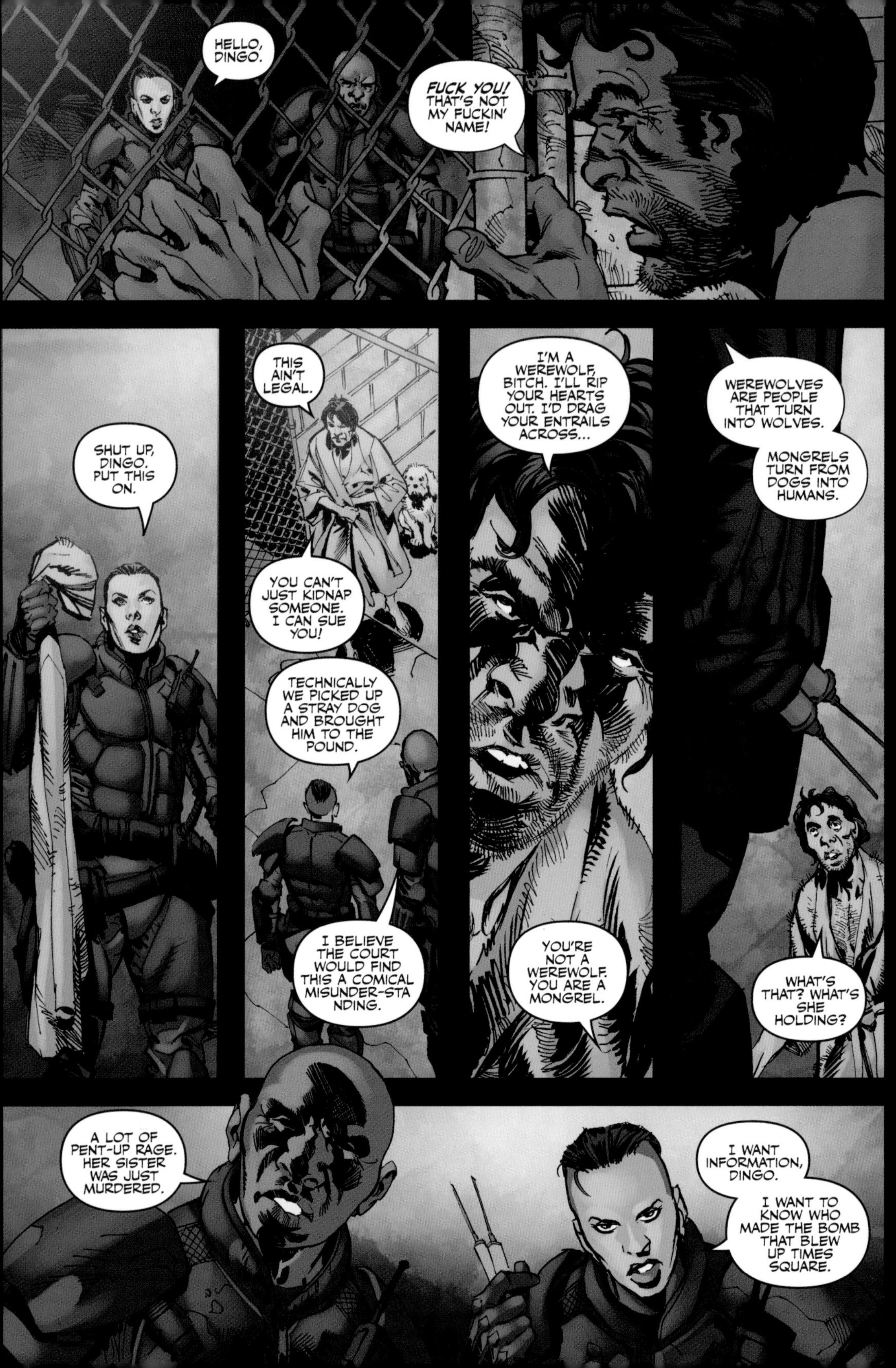
HELLO, DINGO.
FUCK YOU! THAT'S NOT MY FUCKIN' NAME!
SHUT UP, DINGO. PUT THIS ON.
THIS AIN'T LEGAL.
YOU CAN'T JUST KIDNAP SOMEONE. I CAN SUE YOU!
TECHNICALLY WE PICKED UP A STRAY DOG AND BROUGHT HIM TO THE POUND.
I BELIEVE THE COURT WOULD FIND THIS A COMICAL MISUNDER-STANDING.
I'M A WEREWOLF, BITCH. I'LL RIP YOUR HEARTS OUT. I'D DRAG YOUR ENTRAILS ACROSS...
YOU'RE NOT A WEREWOLF. YOU ARE A MONGREL.
WEREWOLVES ARE PEOPLE THAT TURN INTO WOLVES.
MONGRELS TURN FROM DOGS INTO HUMANS.
WHAT'S THAT? WHAT'S SHE HOLDING?
A LOT OF PENT-UP RAGE. HER SISTER WAS JUST MURDERED.
I WANT INFORMATION, DINGO.
I WANT TO KNOW WHO MADE THE BOMB THAT BLEW UP TIMES SQUARE.

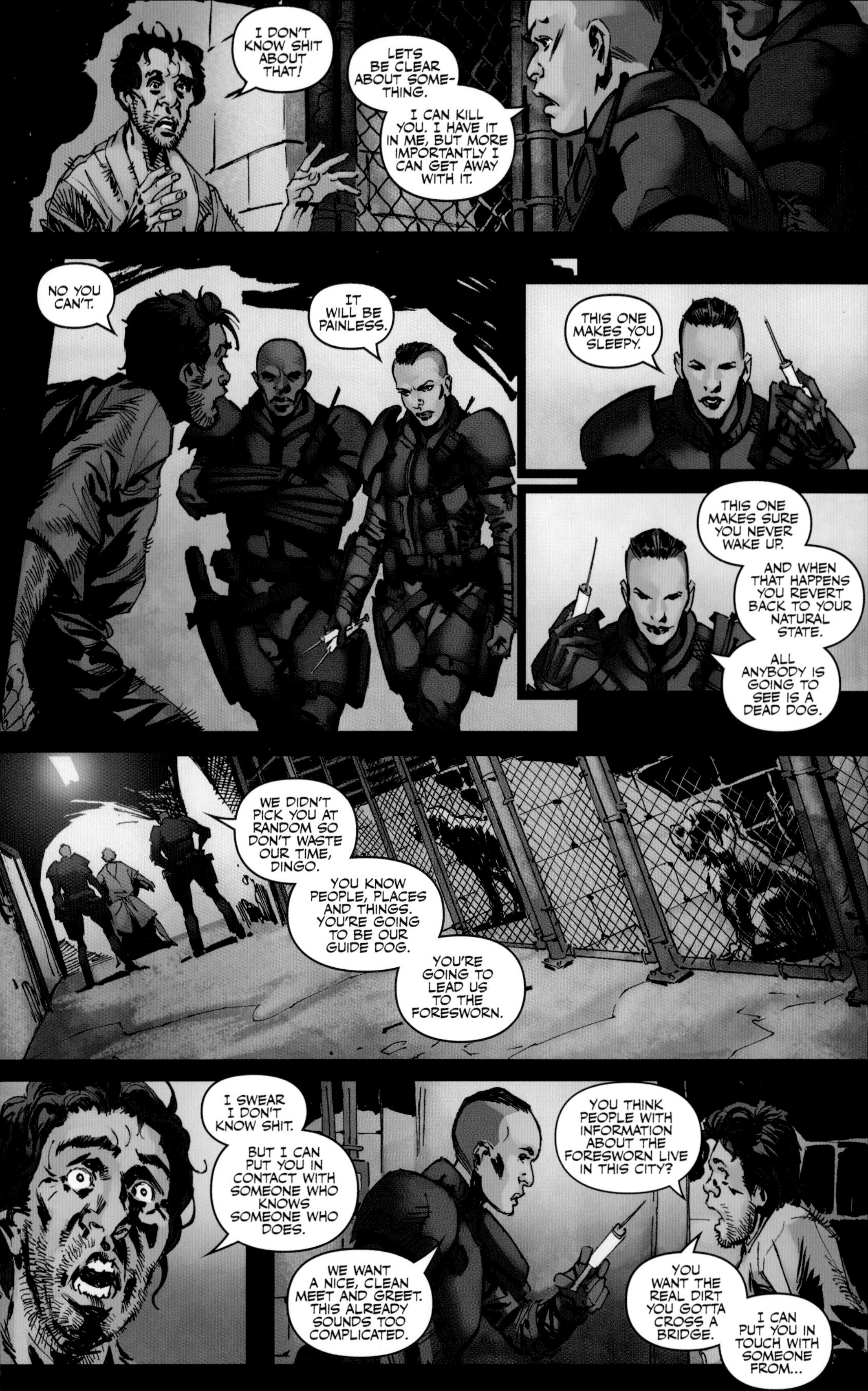
I DON'T KNOW SHIT ABOUT THAT!
LETS BE CLEAR ABOUT SOME-THING.
I CAN KILL YOU. I HAVE IT IN ME, BUT MORE IMPORTANTLY I CAN GET AWAY WITH IT.
NO YOU CAN'T.
IT WILL BE PAINLESS.
THIS ONE MAKES YOU SLEEPY.
THIS ONE MAKES SURE YOU NEVER WAKE UP.
AND WHEN THAT HAPPENS YOU REVERT BACK TO YOUR NATURAL STATE.
ALL ANYBODY IS GOING TO SEE IS A DEAD DOG.
WE DIDN'T PICK YOU AT RANDOM SO DON'T WASTE OUR TIME, DINGO.
YOU KNOW PEOPLE, PLACES AND THINGS. YOU'RE GOING TO BE OUR GUIDE DOG.
YOU'RE GOING TO LEAD US TO THE FORESWORN.
I SWEAR I DON'T KNOW SHIT.
BUT I CAN PUT YOU IN CONTACT WITH SOMEONE WHO KNOWS SOMEONE WHO DOES.
WE WANT A NICE, CLEAN MEET AND GREET. THIS ALREADY SOUNDS TOO COMPLICATED.
YOU THINK PEOPLE WITH INFORMATION ABOUT THE FORESWORN LIVE IN THIS CITY?
YOU WANT THE REAL DIRT YOU GOTTA CROSS A BRIDGE.
I CAN PUT YOU IN TOUCH WITH SOMEONE FROM...

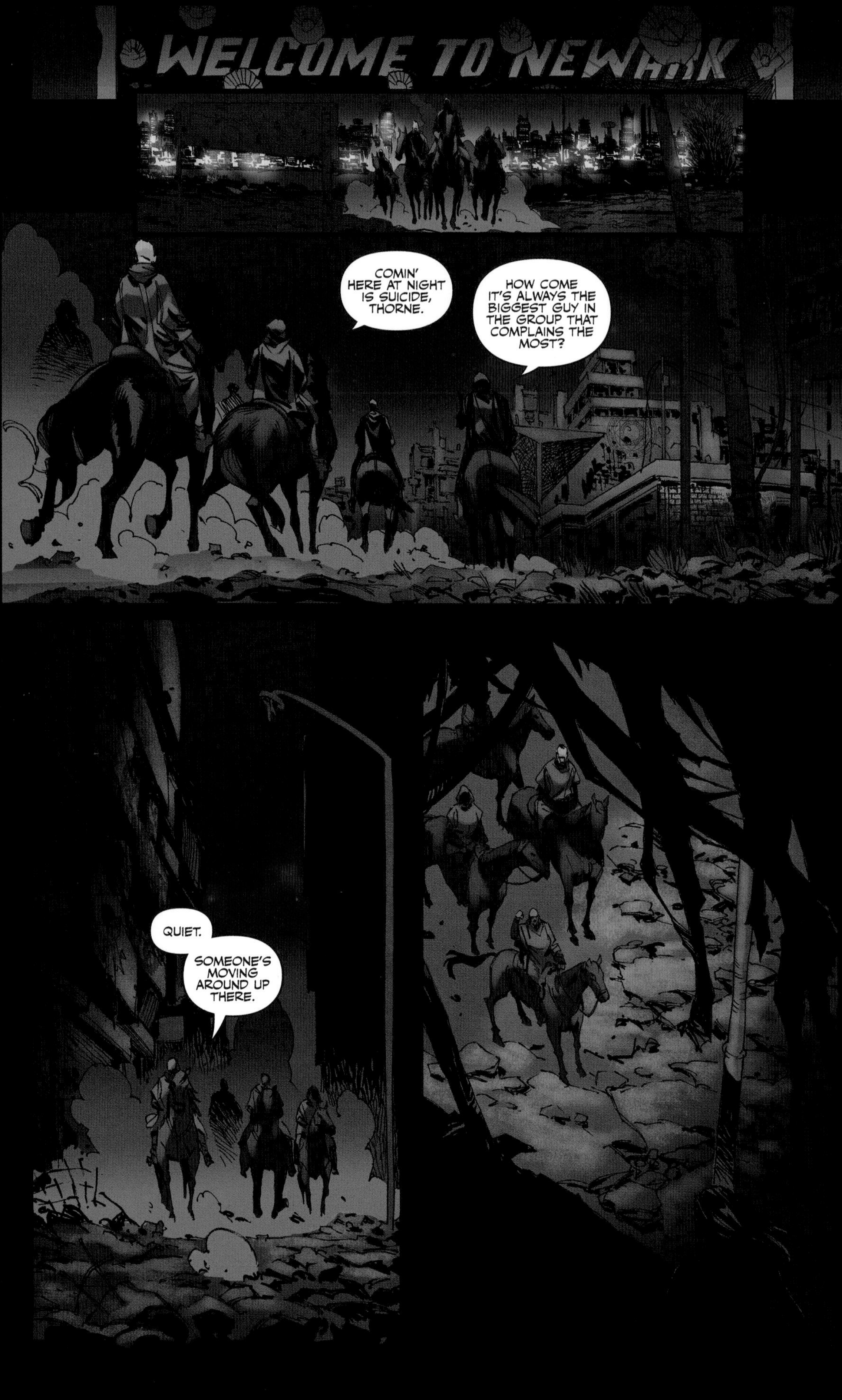
WELCOME TO NEWARK
COMIN' HERE AT NIGHT IS SUICIDE, THORNE.
HOW COME IT'S ALWAYS THE BIGGEST GUY IN THE GROUP THAT COMPLAINS THE MOST?
QUIET.
SOMEONE'S MOVING AROUND UP THERE.

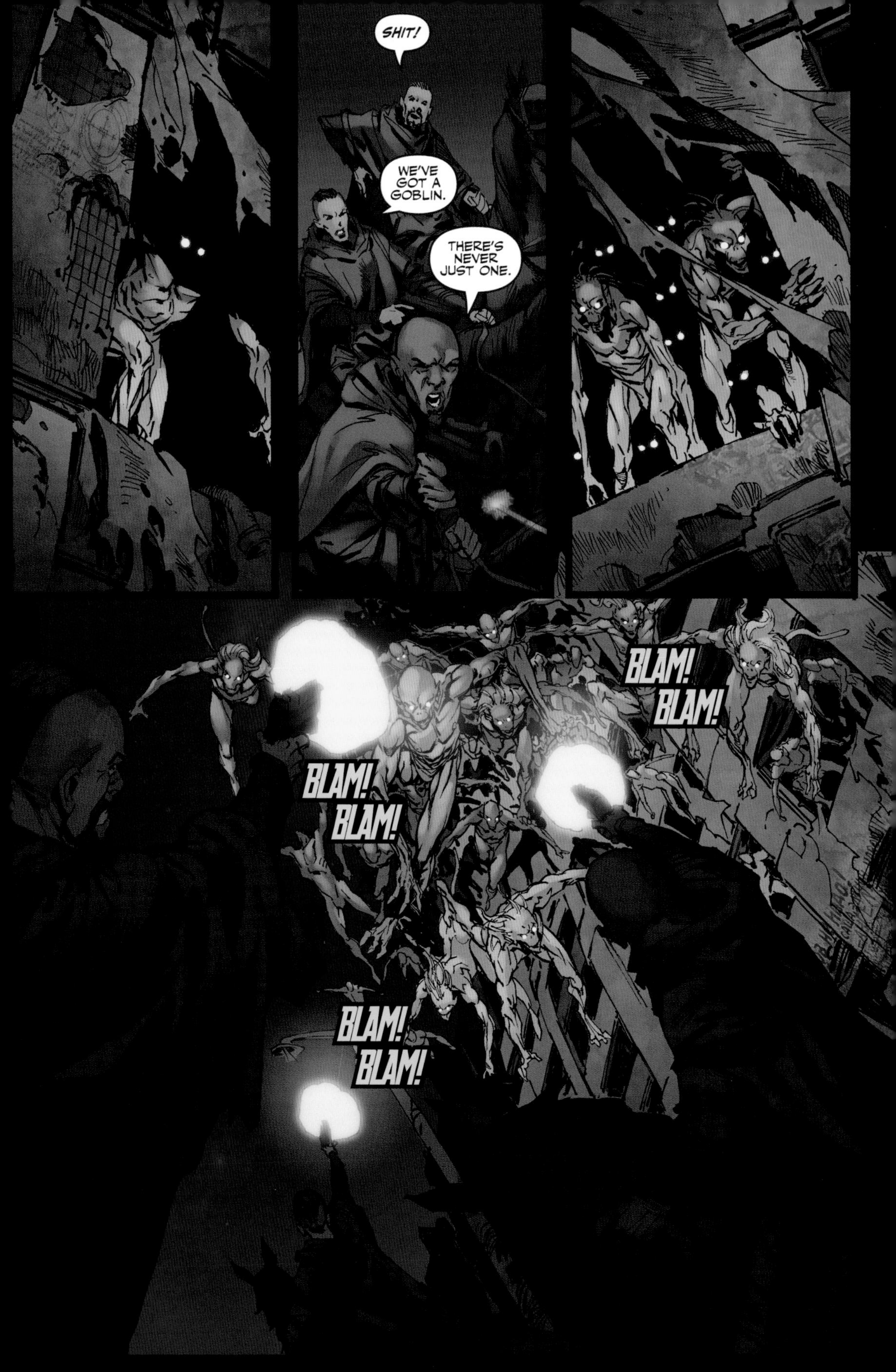
SHIT!
WE'VE GOT A GOBLIN.
THERE'S NEVER JUST ONE.
BLAM! BLAM!
BLAM! BLAM!
BLAM! BLAM!

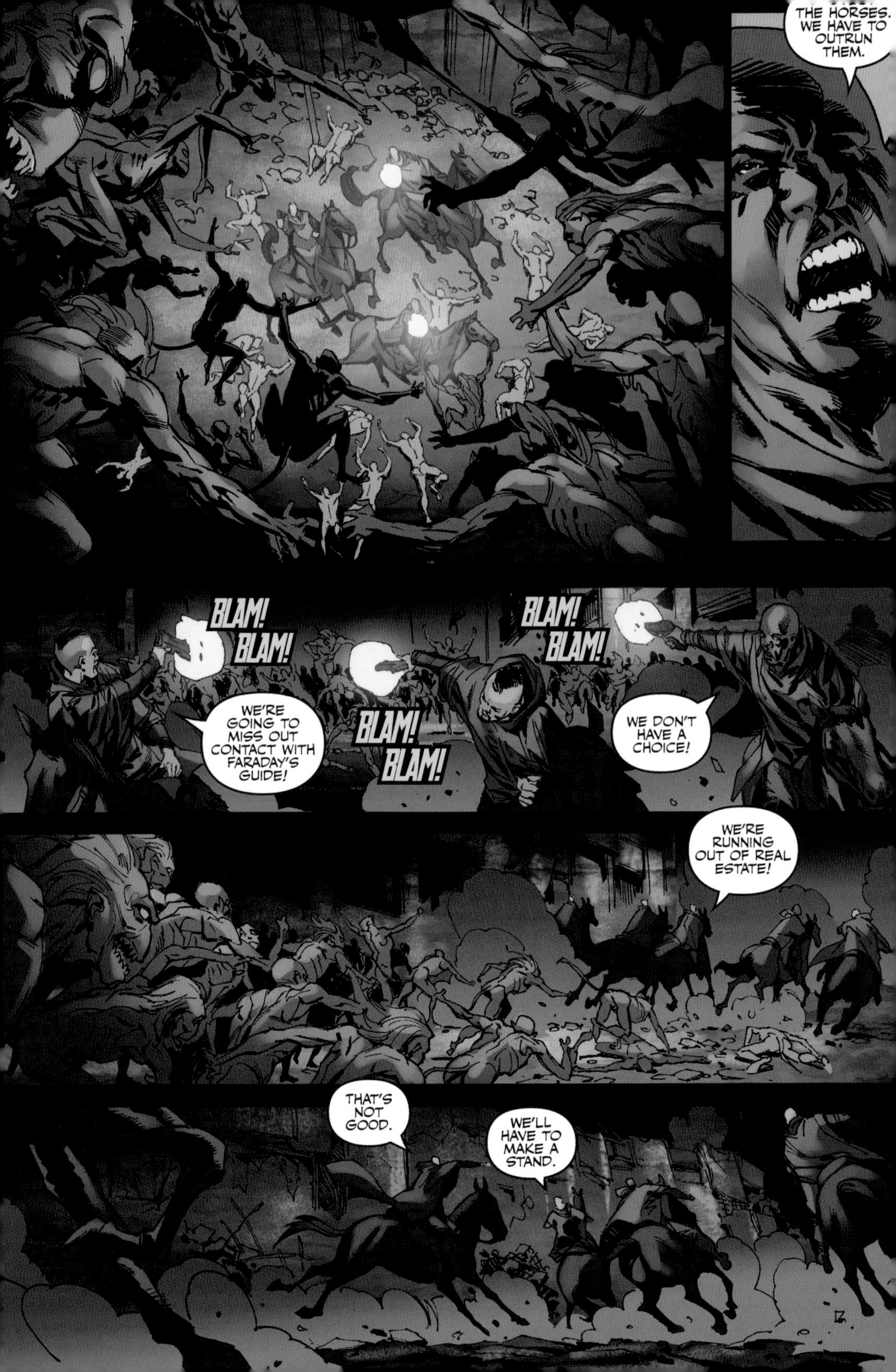
THE HORSES. WE HAVE TO OUTRUN THEM.
BLAM! BLAM!
WE'RE GOING TO MISS OUT CONTACT WITH FARADAY'S GUIDE!
BLAM! BLAM!
BLAM! BLAM!
WE DON'T HAVE A CHOICE!
WE'RE RUNNING OUT OF REAL ESTATE!
THAT'S NOT GOOD.
WE'LL HAVE TO MAKE A STAND.

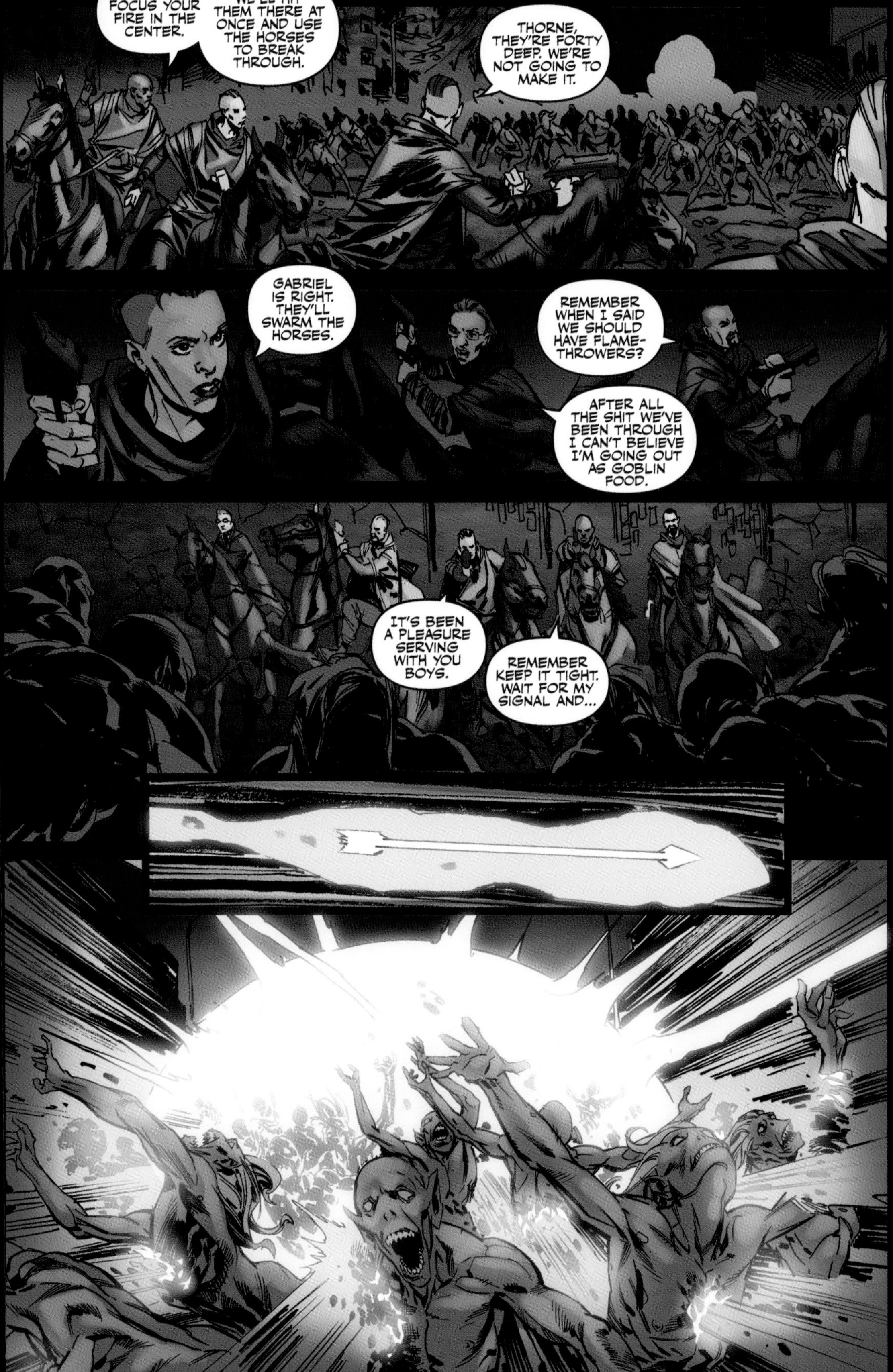
EVERYONE FOCUS YOUR FIRE IN THE CENTER.
WE'LL HIT THEM THERE AT ONCE AND USE THE HORSES TO BREAK THROUGH.
THORNE, THEY'RE FORTY DEEP. WE'RE NOT GOING TO MAKE IT.
GABRIEL IS RIGHT. THEY'LL SWARM THE HORSES.
REMEMBER WHEN I SAID WE SHOULD HAVE FLAME-THROWERS?
AFTER ALL THE SHIT WE'VE BEEN THROUGH I CAN'T BELIEVE I'M GOING OUT AS GOBLIN FOOD.
IT'S BEEN A PLEASURE SERVING WITH YOU BOYS.
REMEMBER KEEP IT TIGHT. WAIT FOR MY SIGNAL AND...

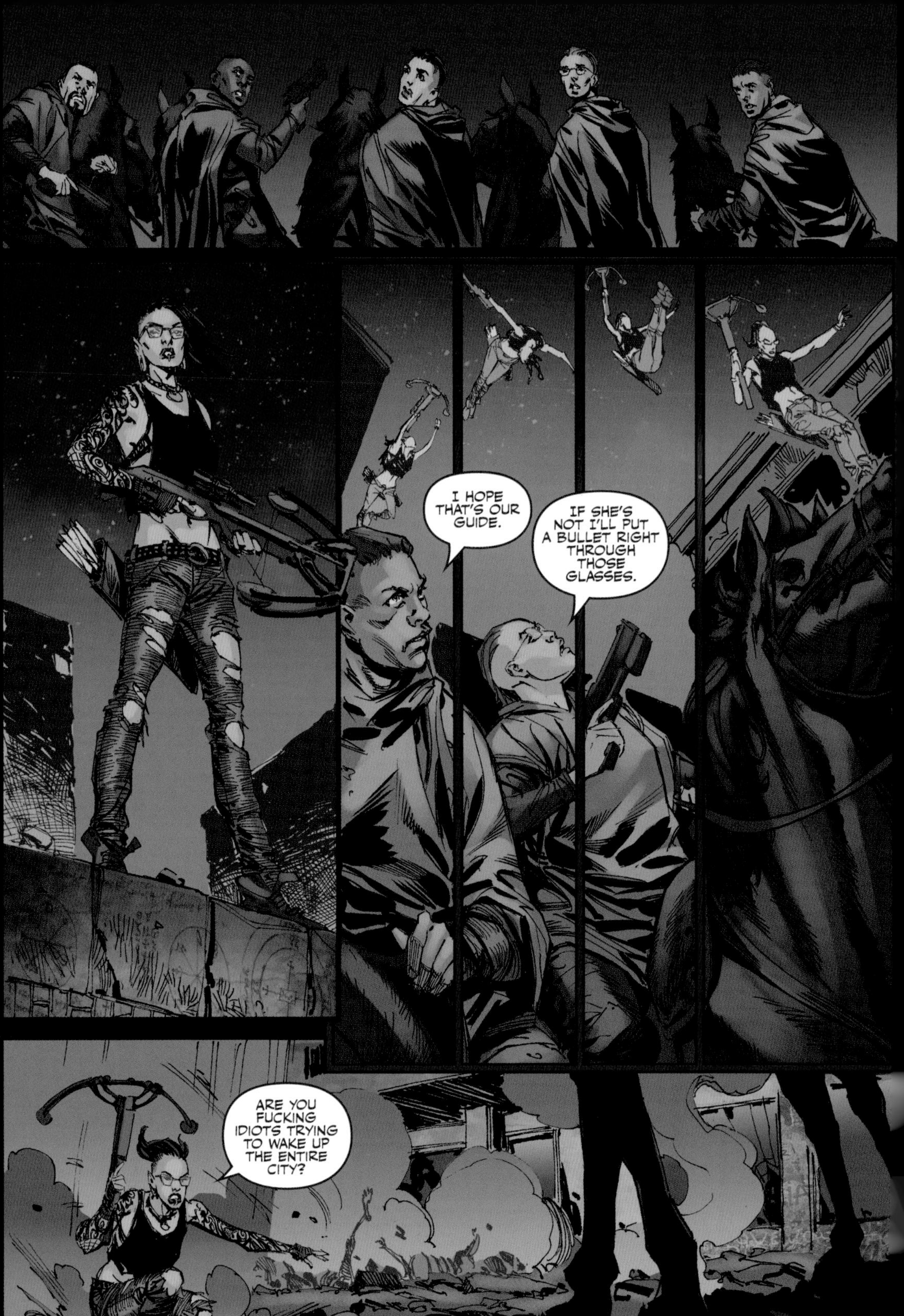
I HOPE THAT'S OUR GUIDE.
IF SHE'S NOT I'LL PUT A BULLET RIGHT THROUGH THOSE GLASSES.
ARE YOU FUCKING IDIOTS TRYING TO WAKE UP THE ENTIRE CITY?

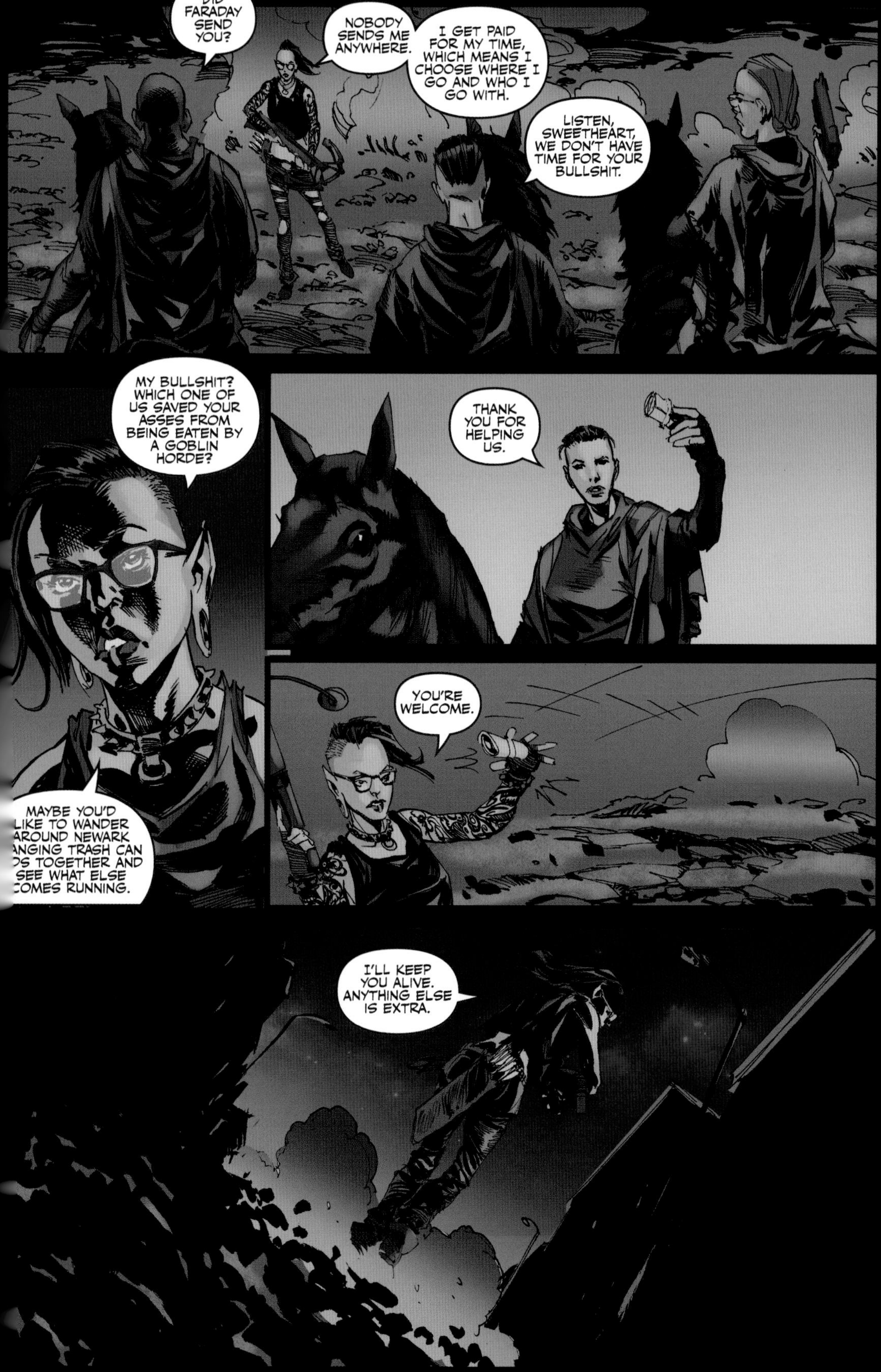
DID FARADAY SEND YOU?
NOBODY SENDS ME ANYWHERE.
I GET PAID FOR MY TIME, WHICH MEANS I CHOOSE WHERE I GO AND WHO I GO WITH.
LISTEN, SWEETHEART, WE DON'T HAVE TIME FOR YOUR BULLSHIT.
MY BULLSHIT? WHICH ONE OF US SAVED YOUR ASSES FROM BEING EATEN BY A GOBLIN HORDE?
MAYBE YOU'D LIKE TO WANDER AROUND NEWARK ANGING TRASH CAN DS TOGETHER AND SEE WHAT ELSE COMES RUNNING.
THANK YOU FOR HELPING US.
YOU'RE WELCOME.
I'LL KEEP YOU ALIVE. ANYTHING ELSE IS EXTRA.

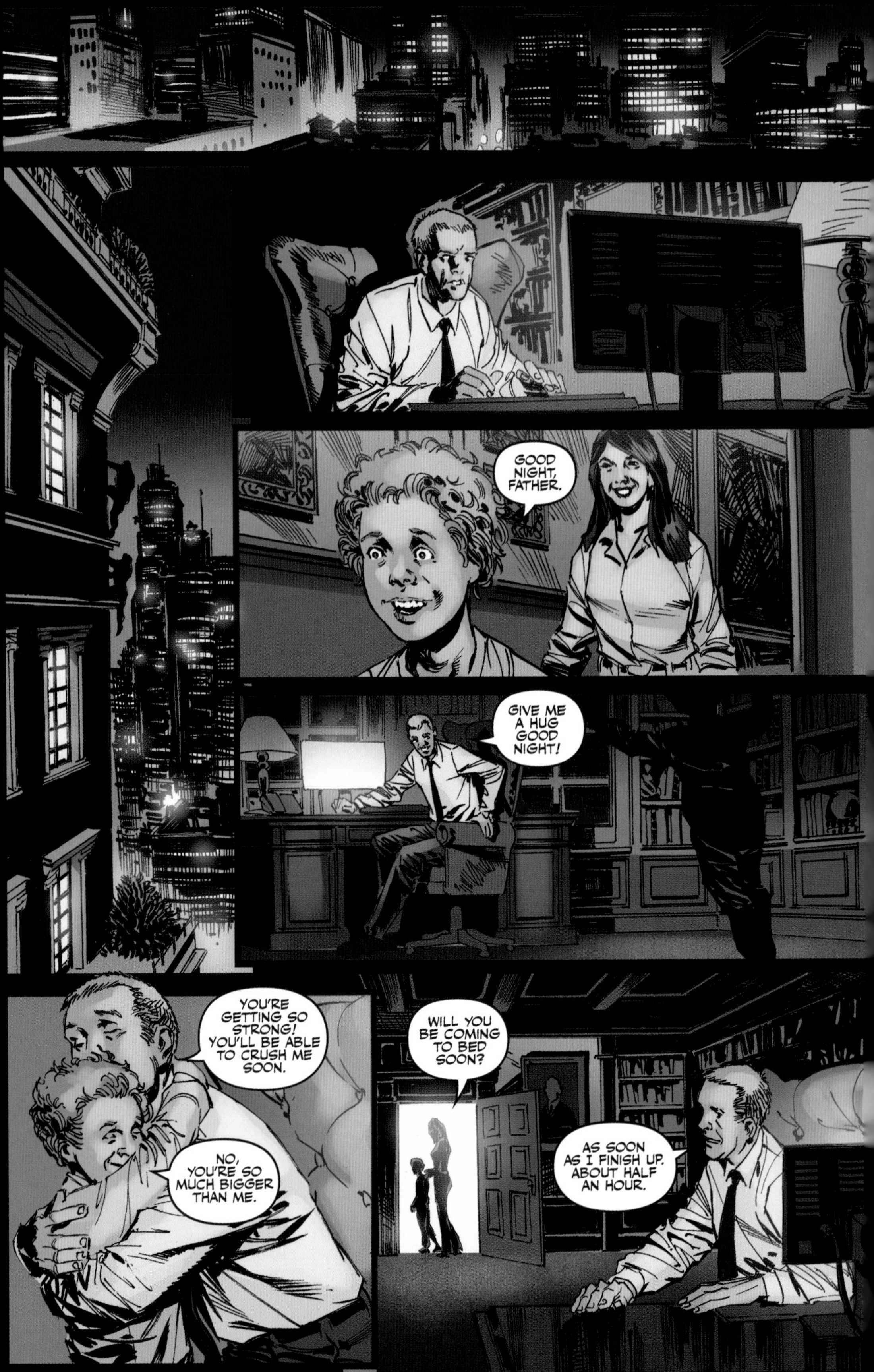
GOOD NIGHT, FATHER.
GIVE ME A HUG GOOD NIGHT!
YOU'RE GETTING SO STRONG! YOU'LL BE ABLE TO CRUSH ME SOON.
NO, YOU'RE SO MUCH BIGGER THAN ME.
WILL YOU BE COMING TO BED SOON?
AS SOON AS I FINISH UP. ABOUT HALF AN HOUR.

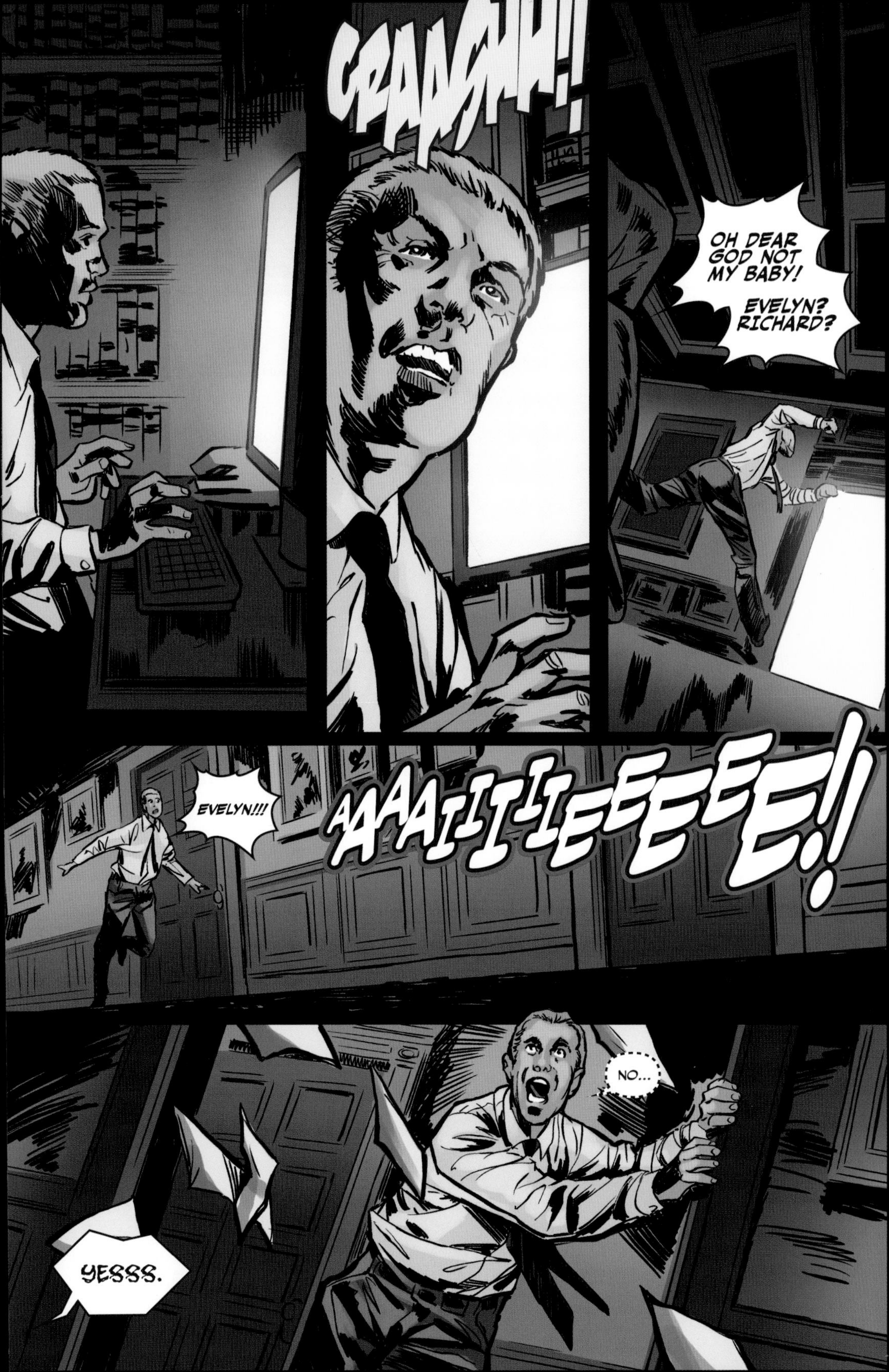
CRAASHH!!
OH DEAR GOD NOT MY BABY!
EVELYN? RICHARD?
EVELYN!!!
AAAIIIIEEEEEE!!
NO...
YESSS.

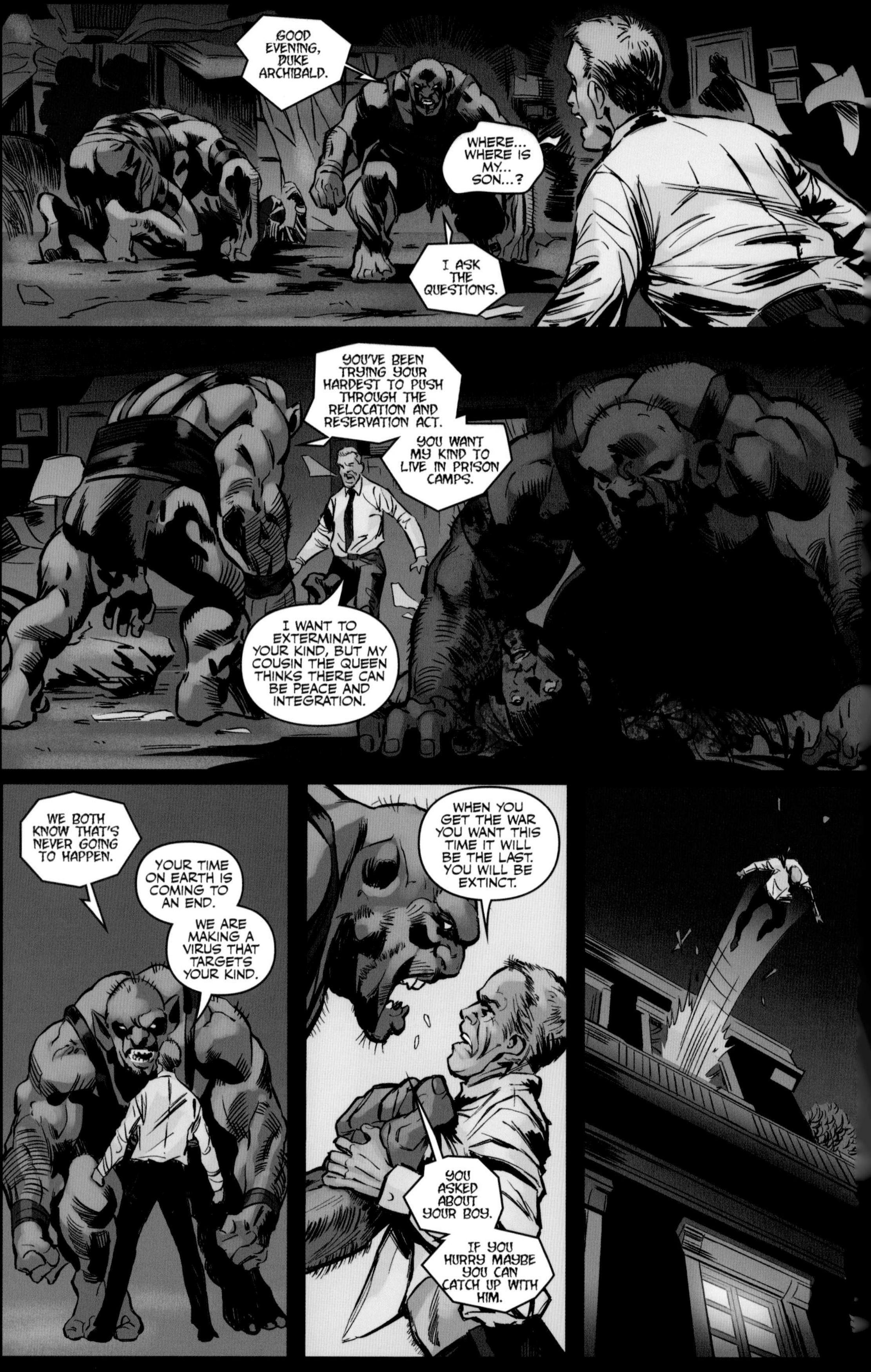
GOOD EVENING, DUKE ARCHIBALD.
WHERE... WHERE IS MY... SON...?
I ASK THE QUESTIONS.
YOU'VE BEEN TRYING YOUR HARDEST TO PUSH THROUGH THE RELOCATION AND RESERVATION ACT.
YOU WANT MY KIND TO LIVE IN PRISON CAMPS.
I WANT TO EXTERMINATE YOUR KIND, BUT MY COUSIN THE QUEEN THINKS THERE CAN BE PEACE AND INTEGRATION.
WE BOTH KNOW THAT'S NEVER GOING TO HAPPEN.
YOUR TIME ON EARTH IS COMING TO AN END.
WE ARE MAKING A VIRUS THAT TARGETS YOUR KIND.
WHEN YOU GET THE WAR YOU WANT THIS TIME IT WILL BE THE LAST. YOU WILL BE EXTINCT.
YOU ASKED ABOUT YOUR BOY.
IF YOU HURRY MAYBE YOU CAN CATCH UP WITH HIM.

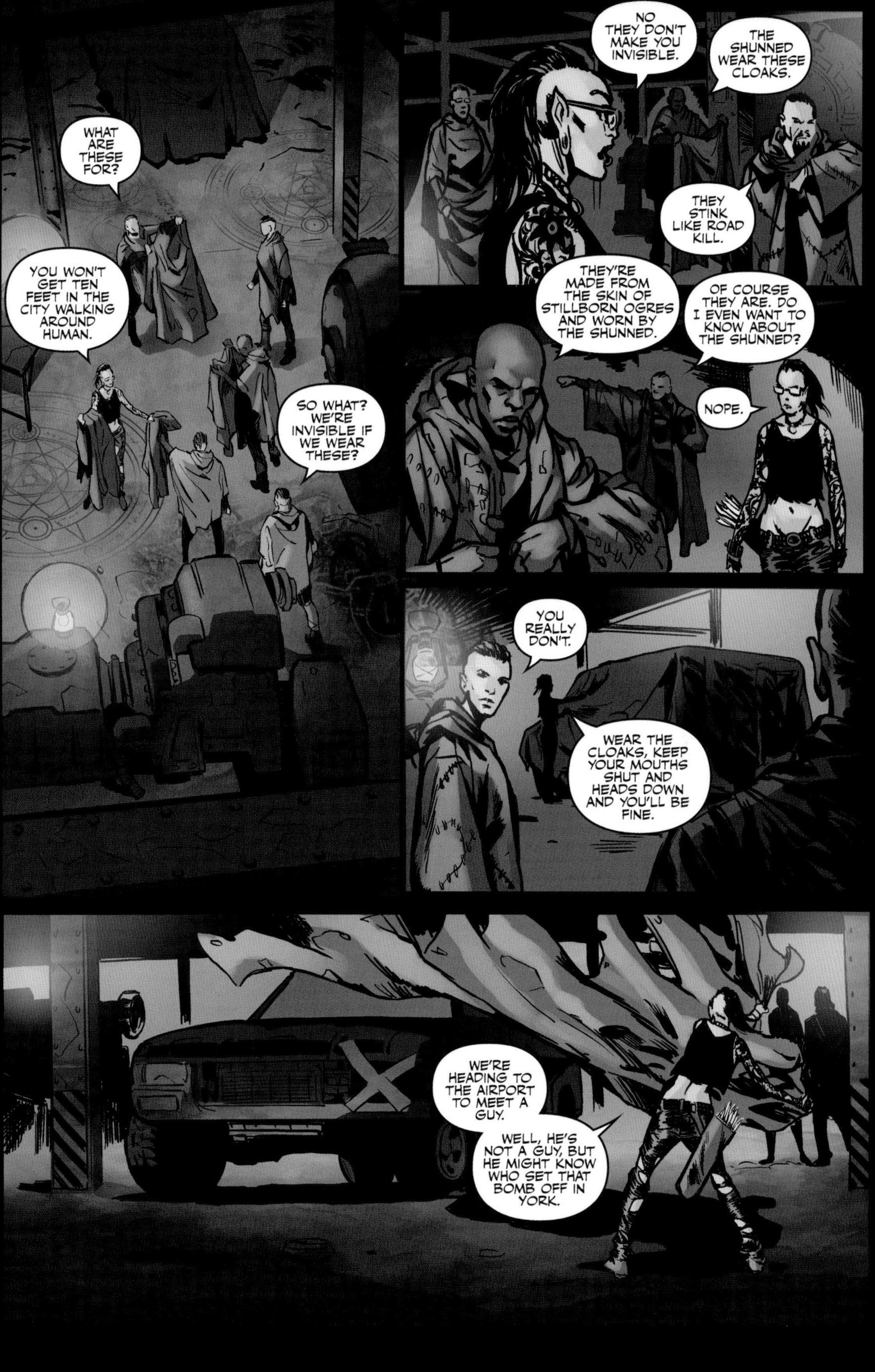
WHAT ARE THESE FOR?
YOU WON'T GET TEN FEET IN THE CITY WALKING AROUND HUMAN.
SO WHAT? WE'RE INVISIBLE IF WE WEAR THESE?
NO THEY DON'T MAKE YOU INVISIBLE.
THE SHUNNED WEAR THESE CLOAKS.
THEY STINK LIKE ROAD KILL.
THEY'RE MADE FROM THE SKIN OF STILLBORN OGRES AND WORN BY THE SHUNNED.
OF COURSE THEY ARE. DO I EVEN WANT TO KNOW ABOUT THE SHUNNED?
NOPE.
YOU REALLY DON'T.
WEAR THE CLOAKS, KEEP YOUR MOUTHS SHUT AND HEADS DOWN AND YOU'LL BE FINE.
WE'RE HEADING TO THE AIRPORT TO MEET A GUY.
WELL, HE'S NOT A GUY, BUT HE MIGHT KNOW WHO SET THAT BOMB OFF IN YORK.

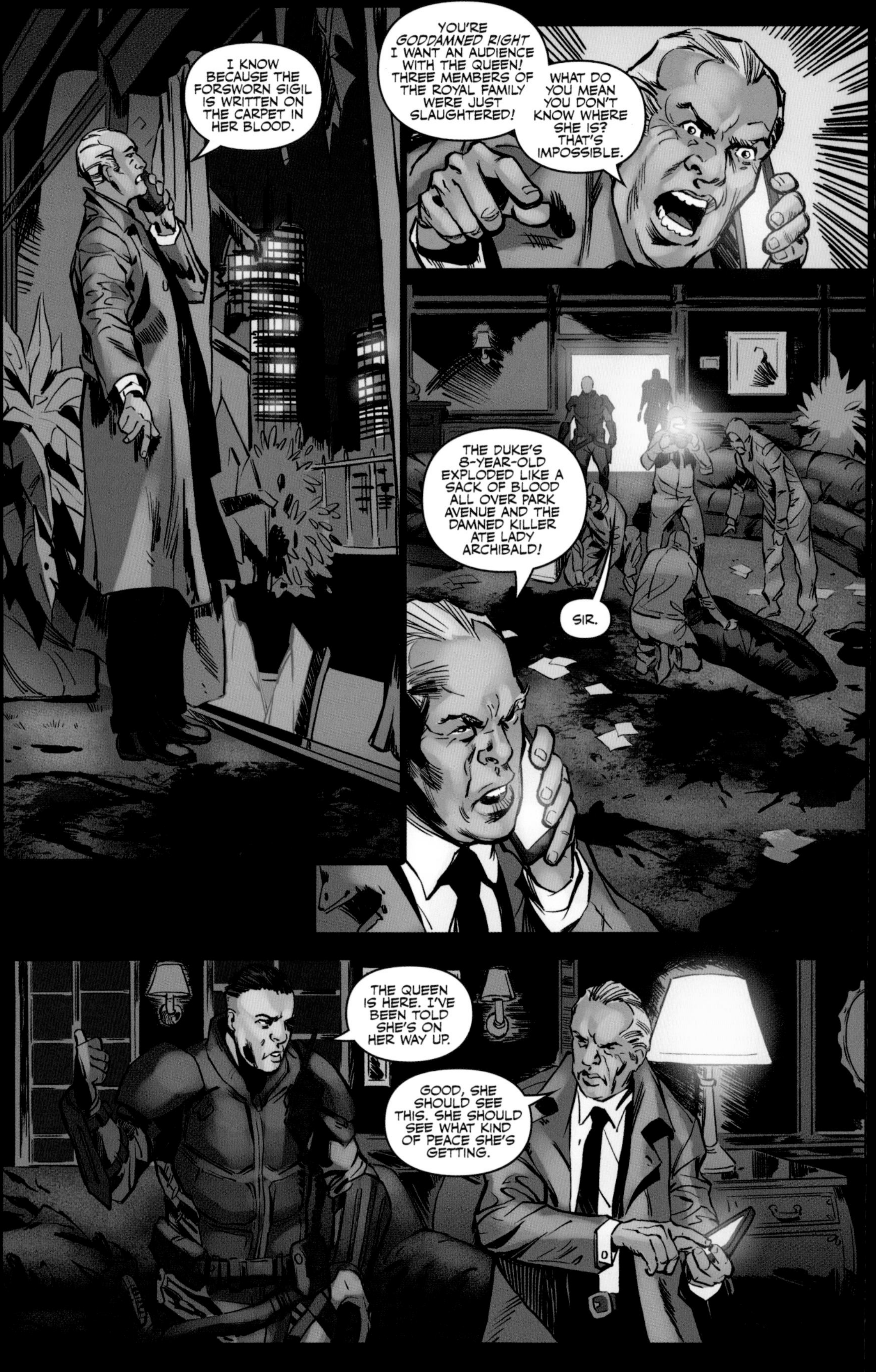
I KNOW BECAUSE THE FORSWORN SIGIL IS WRITTEN ON THE CARPET IN HER BLOOD.
YOU'RE GODDAMNED RIGHT I WANT AN AUDIENCE WITH THE QUEEN! THREE MEMBERS OF THE ROYAL FAMILY WERE JUST SLAUGHTERED!
WHAT DO YOU MEAN YOU DON'T KNOW WHERE SHE IS? THAT'S IMPOSSIBLE.
THE DUKE'S 8-YEAR-OLD EXPLODED LIKE A SACK OF BLOOD ALL OVER PARK AVENUE AND THE DAMNED KILLER ATE LADY ARCHIBALD!
SIR.
THE QUEEN IS HERE. I'VE BEEN TOLD SHE'S ON HER WAY UP.
GOOD, SHE SHOULD SEE THIS. SHE SHOULD SEE WHAT KIND OF PEACE SHE'S GETTING.

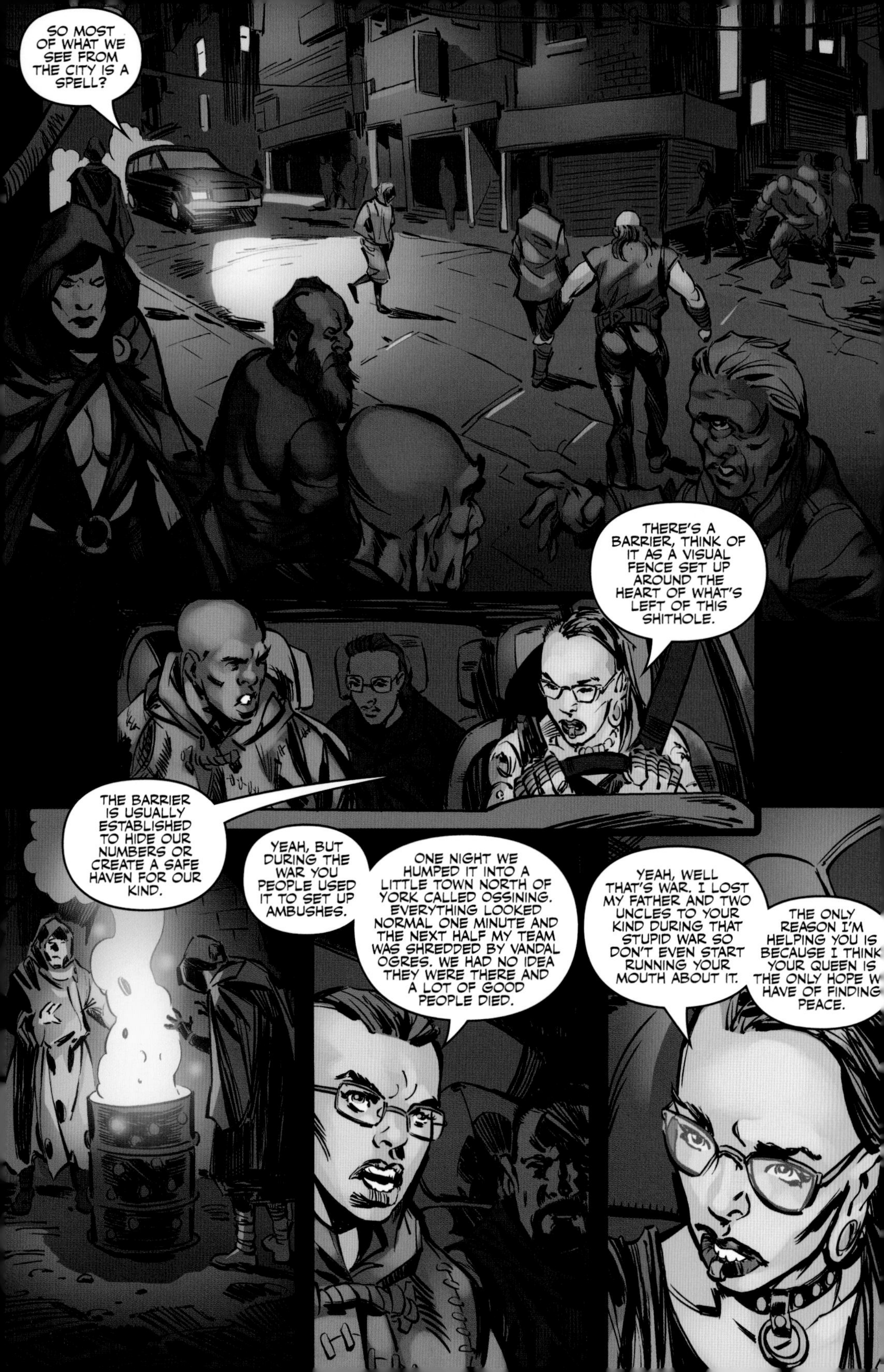
SO MOST OF WHAT WE SEE FROM THE CITY IS A SPELL?
THERE'S A BARRIER, THINK OF IT AS A VISUAL FENCE SET UP AROUND THE HEART OF WHAT'S LEFT OF THIS SHITHOLE.
THE BARRIER IS USUALLY ESTABLISHED TO HIDE OUR NUMBERS OR CREATE A SAFE HAVEN FOR OUR KIND.
YEAH, BUT DURING THE WAR YOU PEOPLE USED IT TO SET UP AMBUSHES.
ONE NIGHT WE HUMPED IT INTO A LITTLE TOWN NORTH OF YORK CALLED OSSINING. EVERYTHING LOOKED NORMAL ONE MINUTE AND THE NEXT HALF MY TEAM WAS SHREDDED BY VANDAL OGRES. WE HAD NO IDEA THEY WERE THERE AND A LOT OF GOOD PEOPLE DIED.
YEAH, WELL THAT'S WAR. I LOST MY FATHER AND TWO UNCLES TO YOUR KIND DURING THAT STUPID WAR SO DON'T EVEN START RUNNING YOUR MOUTH ABOUT IT.
THE ONLY REASON I'M HELPING YOU IS BECAUSE I THINK YOUR QUEEN IS THE ONLY HOPE W HAVE OF FINDING PEACE.

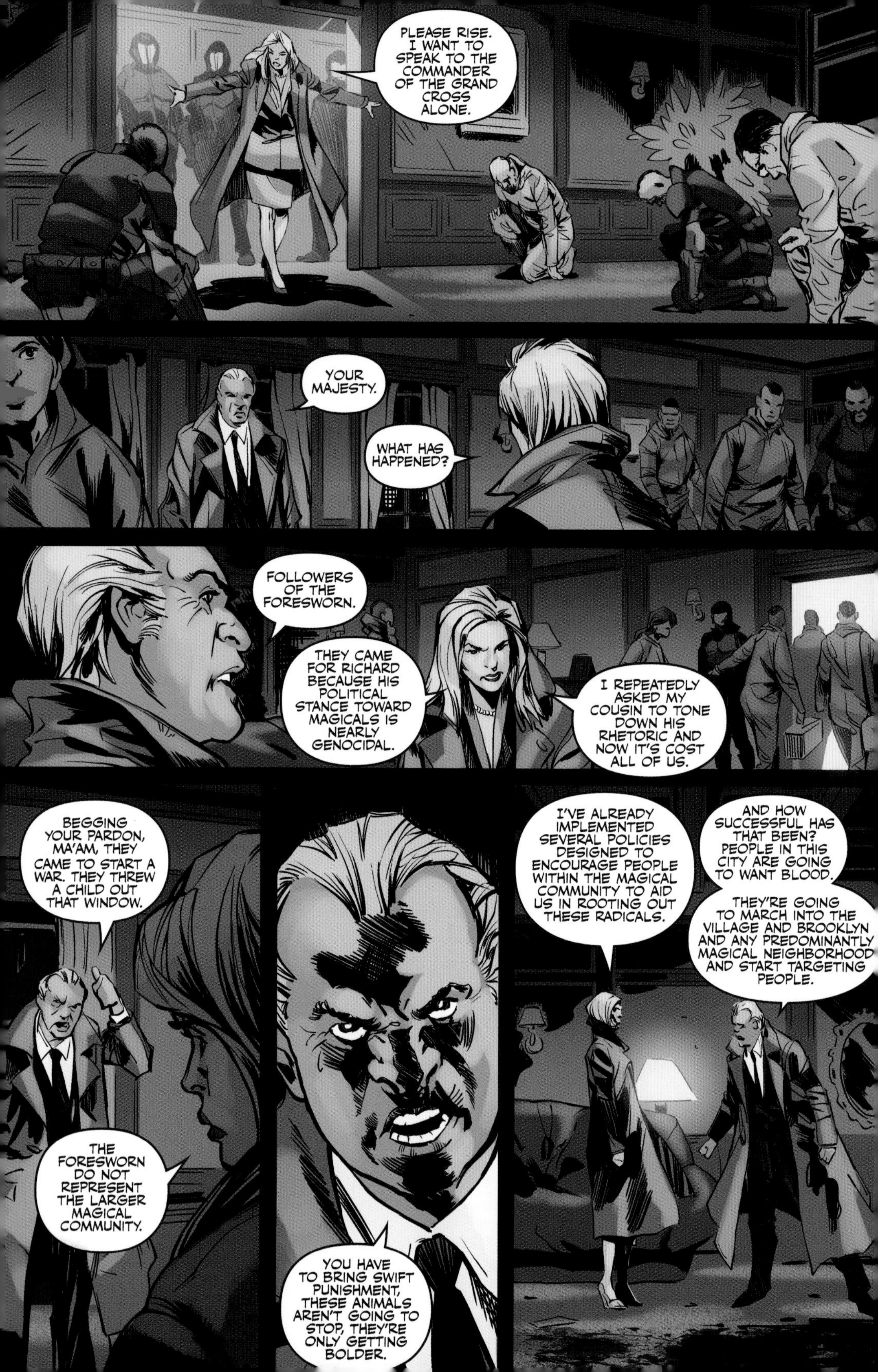
PLEASE RISE. I WANT TO SPEAK TO THE COMMANDER OF THE GRAND CROSS ALONE.
YOUR MAJESTY.
WHAT HAS HAPPENED?
FOLLOWERS OF THE FORESWORN.
THEY CAME FOR RICHARD BECAUSE HIS POLITICAL STANCE TOWARD MAGICALS IS NEARLY GENOCIDAL.
I REPEATEDLY ASKED MY COUSIN TO TONE DOWN HIS RHETORIC AND NOW IT'S COST ALL OF US.
BEGGING YOUR PARDON, MA'AM, THEY CAME TO START A WAR. THEY THREW A CHILD OUT THAT WINDOW.
THE FORESWORN DO NOT REPRESENT THE LARGER MAGICAL COMMUNITY.
YOU HAVE TO BRING SWIFT PUNISHMENT, THESE ANIMALS AREN'T GOING TO STOP, THEY'RE ONLY GETTING BOLDER.
I'VE ALREADY IMPLEMENTED SEVERAL POLICIES DESIGNED TO ENCOURAGE PEOPLE WITHIN THE MAGICAL COMMUNITY TO AID US IN ROOTING OUT THESE RADICALS.
AND HOW SUCCESSFUL HAS THAT BEEN? PEOPLE IN THIS CITY ARE GOING TO WANT BLOOD.
THEY'RE GOING TO MARCH INTO THE VILLAGE AND BROOKLYN AND ANY PREDOMINANTLY MAGICAL NEIGHBORHOOD AND START TARGETING PEOPLE.

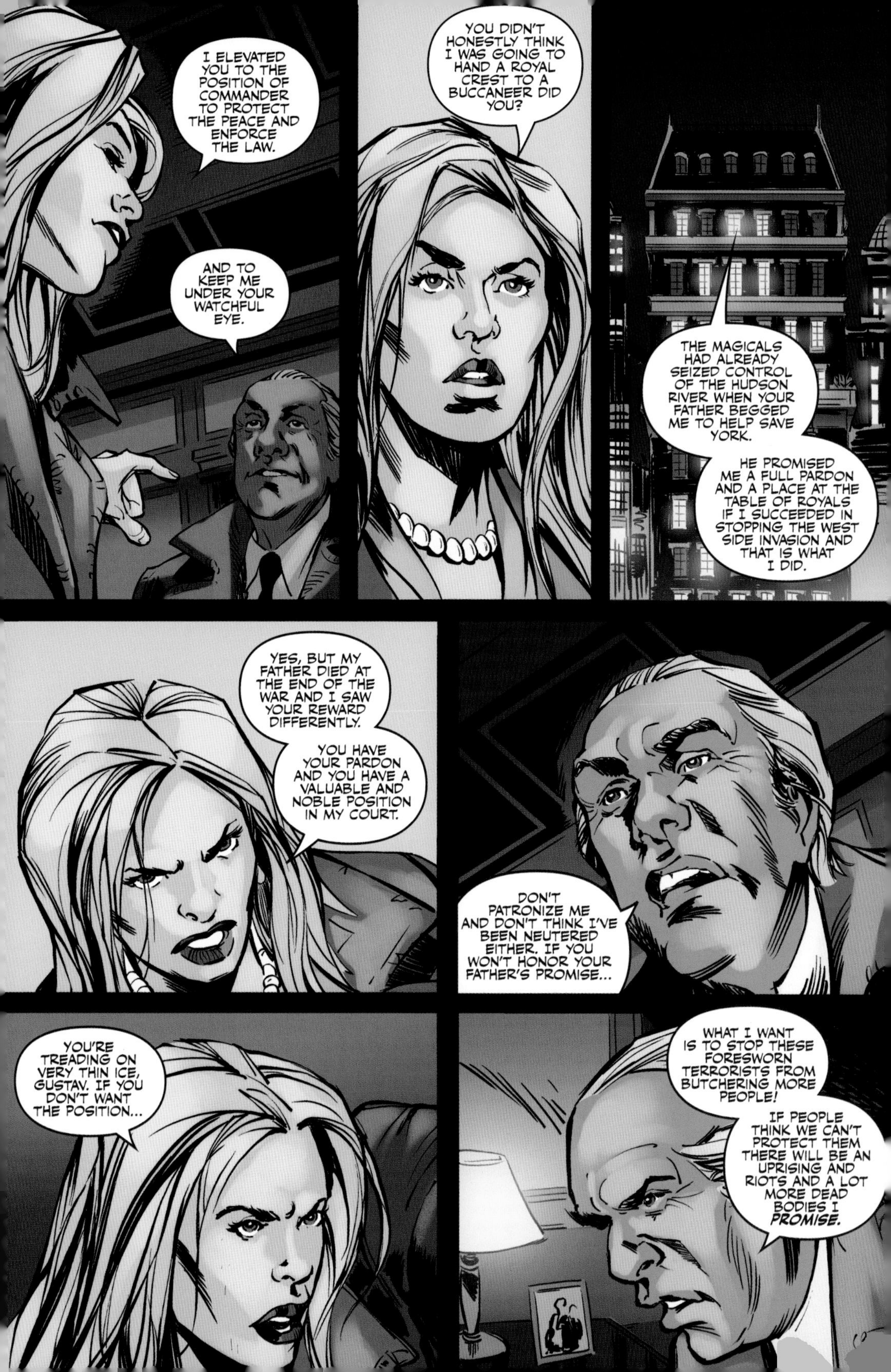
I ELEVATED YOU TO THE POSITION OF COMMANDER TO PROTECT THE PEACE AND ENFORCE THE LAW.
AND TO KEEP ME UNDER YOUR WATCHFUL EYE.
YOU DIDN'T HONESTLY THINK I WAS GOING TO HAND A ROYAL CREST TO A BUCCANEER DID YOU?
THE MAGICALS HAD ALREADY SEIZED CONTROL OF THE HUDSON RIVER WHEN YOUR FATHER BEGGED ME TO HELP SAVE YORK.
HE PROMISED ME A FULL PARDON AND A PLACE AT THE TABLE OF ROYALS IF I SUCCEEDED IN STOPPING THE WEST SIDE INVASION AND THAT IS WHAT I DID.
YES, BUT MY FATHER DIED AT THE END OF THE WAR AND I SAW YOUR REWARD DIFFERENTLY.
YOU HAVE YOUR PARDON AND YOU HAVE A VALUABLE AND NOBLE POSITION IN MY COURT.
DON'T PATRONIZE ME AND DON'T THINK I'VE BEEN NEUTERED EITHER. IF YOU WON'T HONOR YOUR FATHER'S PROMISE...
YOU'RE TREADING ON VERY THIN ICE, GUSTAV. IF YOU DON'T WANT THE POSITION...
WHAT I WANT IS TO STOP THESE FORESWORN TERRORISTS FROM BUTCHERING MORE PEOPLE!
IF PEOPLE THINK WE CAN'T PROTECT THEM THERE WILL BE AN UPRISING AND RIOTS AND A LOT MORE DEAD BODIES I ***PROMISE.***

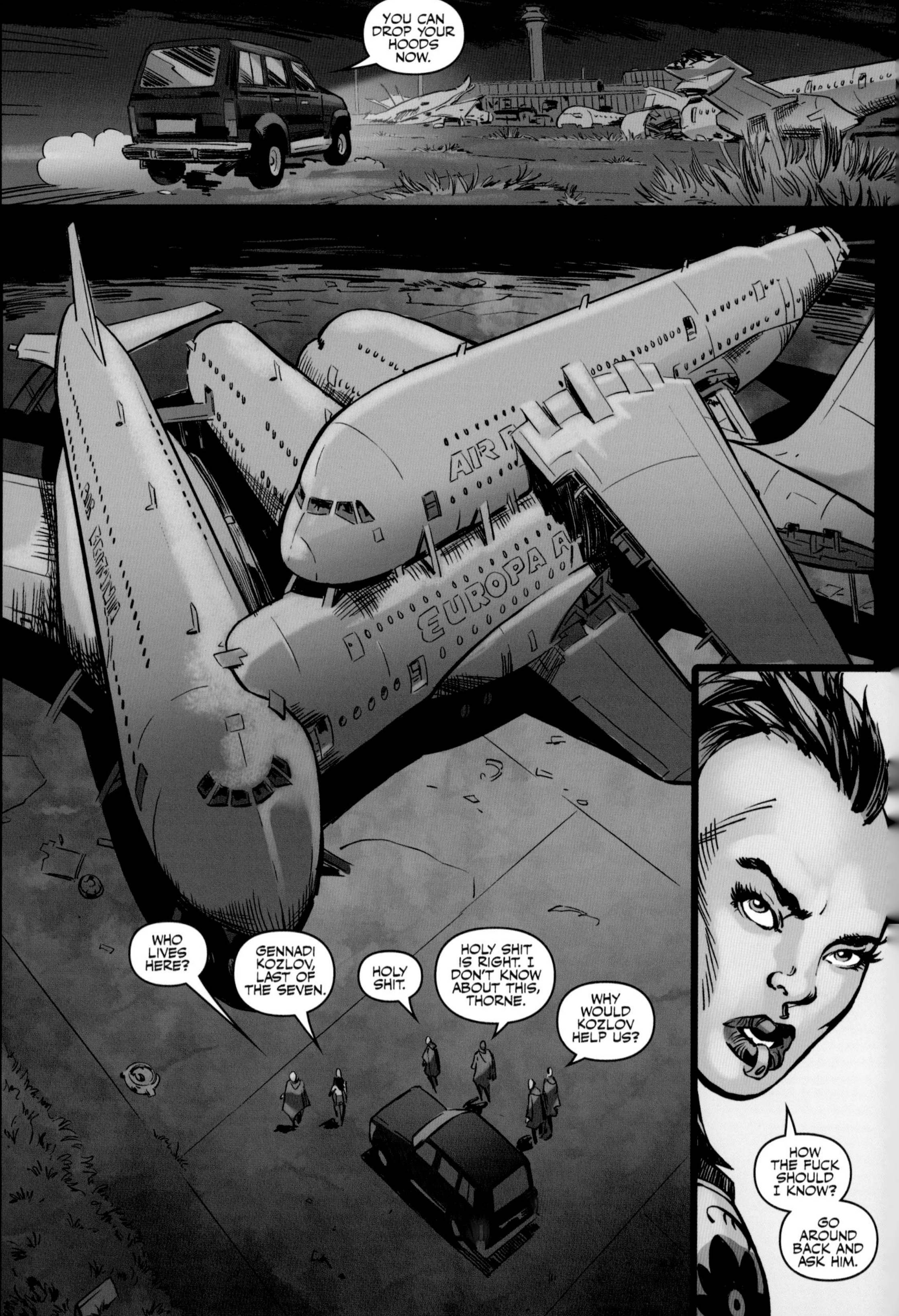
YOU CAN DROP YOUR HOODS NOW.
WHO LIVES HERE?
GENNADI KOZLOV, LAST OF THE SEVEN.
HOLY SHIT.
HOLY SHIT IS RIGHT. I DON'T KNOW ABOUT THIS, THORNE.
WHY WOULD KOZLOV HELP US?
HOW THE FUCK SHOULD I KNOW?
GO AROUND BACK AND ASK HIM.

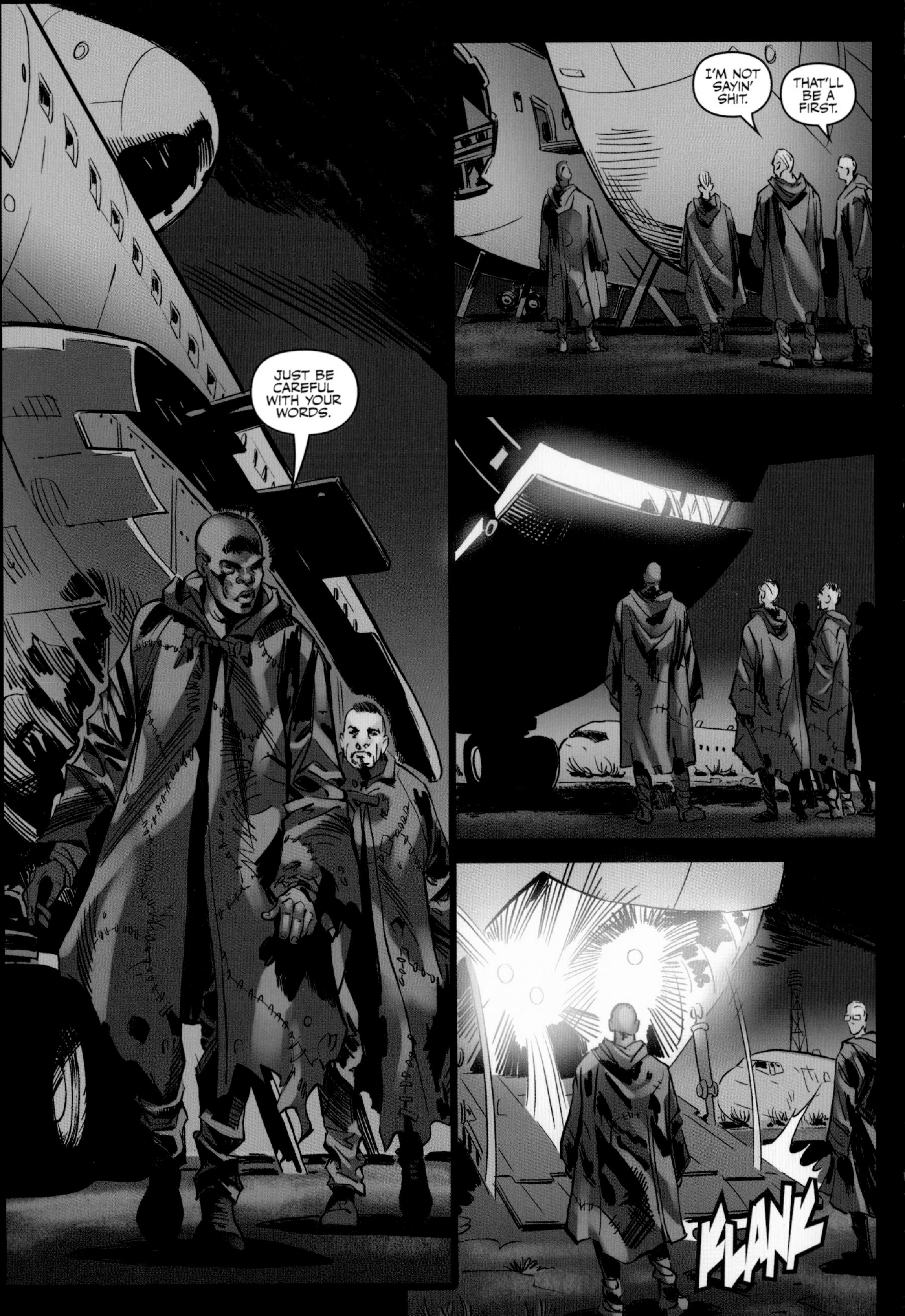
JUST BE CAREFUL WITH YOUR WORDS.
I'M NOT SAYIN' SHIT.
THAT'LL BE A FIRST.
KLANK

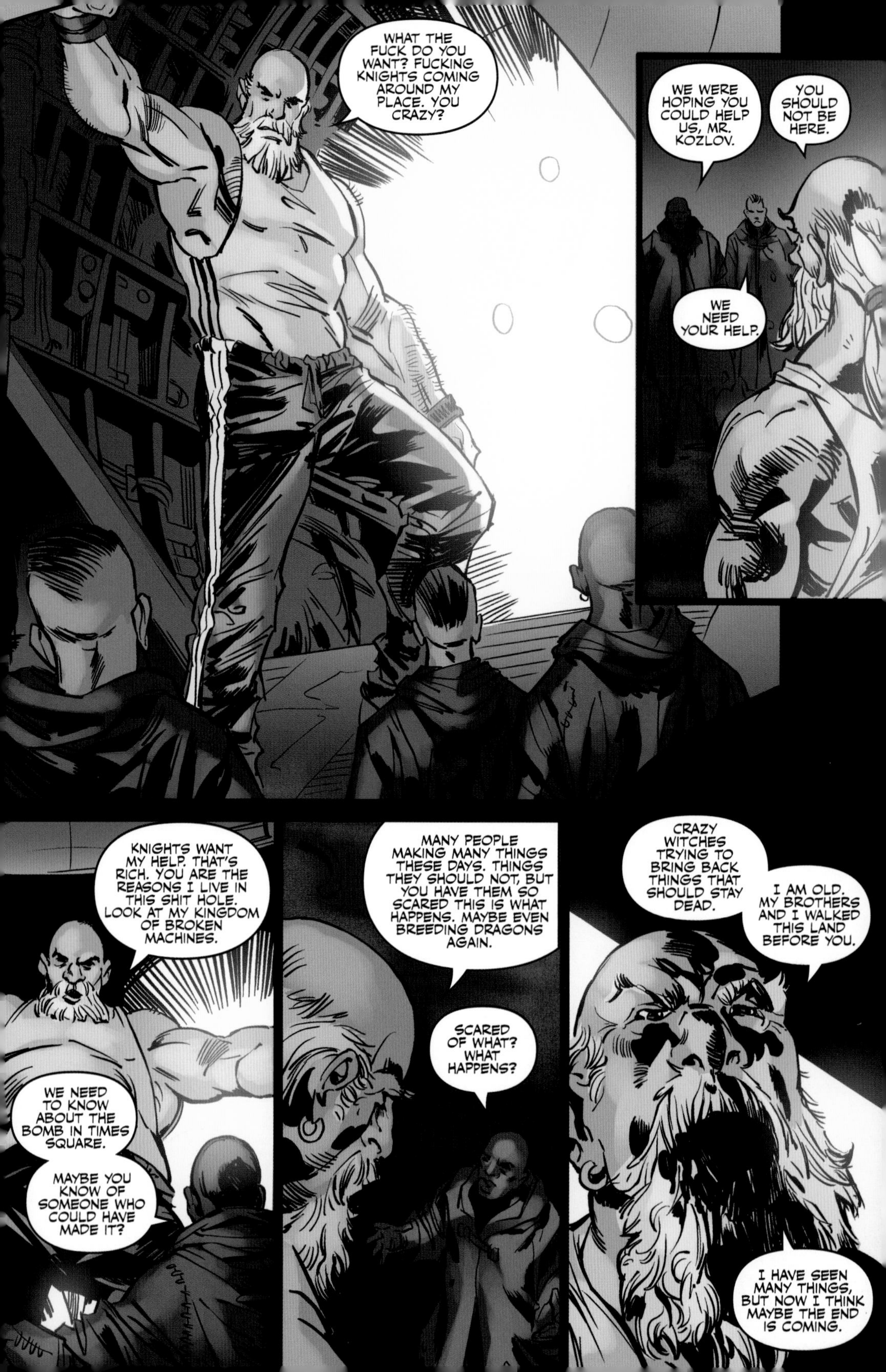
WHAT THE FUCK DO YOU WANT? FUCKING KNIGHTS COMING AROUND MY PLACE. YOU CRAZY?
WE WERE HOPING YOU COULD HELP US, MR. KOZLOV.
YOU SHOULD NOT BE HERE.
WE NEED YOUR HELP.
KNIGHTS WANT MY HELP. THAT'S RICH. YOU ARE THE REASONS I LIVE IN THIS SHIT HOLE. LOOK AT MY KINGDOM OF BROKEN MACHINES.
WE NEED TO KNOW ABOUT THE BOMB IN TIMES SQUARE.
MAYBE YOU KNOW OF SOMEONE WHO COULD HAVE MADE IT?
MANY PEOPLE MAKING MANY THINGS THESE DAYS. THINGS THEY SHOULD NOT, BUT YOU HAVE THEM SO SCARED THIS IS WHAT HAPPENS. MAYBE EVEN BREEDING DRAGONS AGAIN.
SCARED OF WHAT? WHAT HAPPENS?
CRAZY WITCHES TRYING TO BRING BACK THINGS THAT SHOULD STAY DEAD.
I AM OLD. MY BROTHERS AND I WALKED THIS LAND BEFORE YOU.
I HAVE SEEN MANY THINGS, BUT NOW I THINK MAYBE THE END IS COMING.

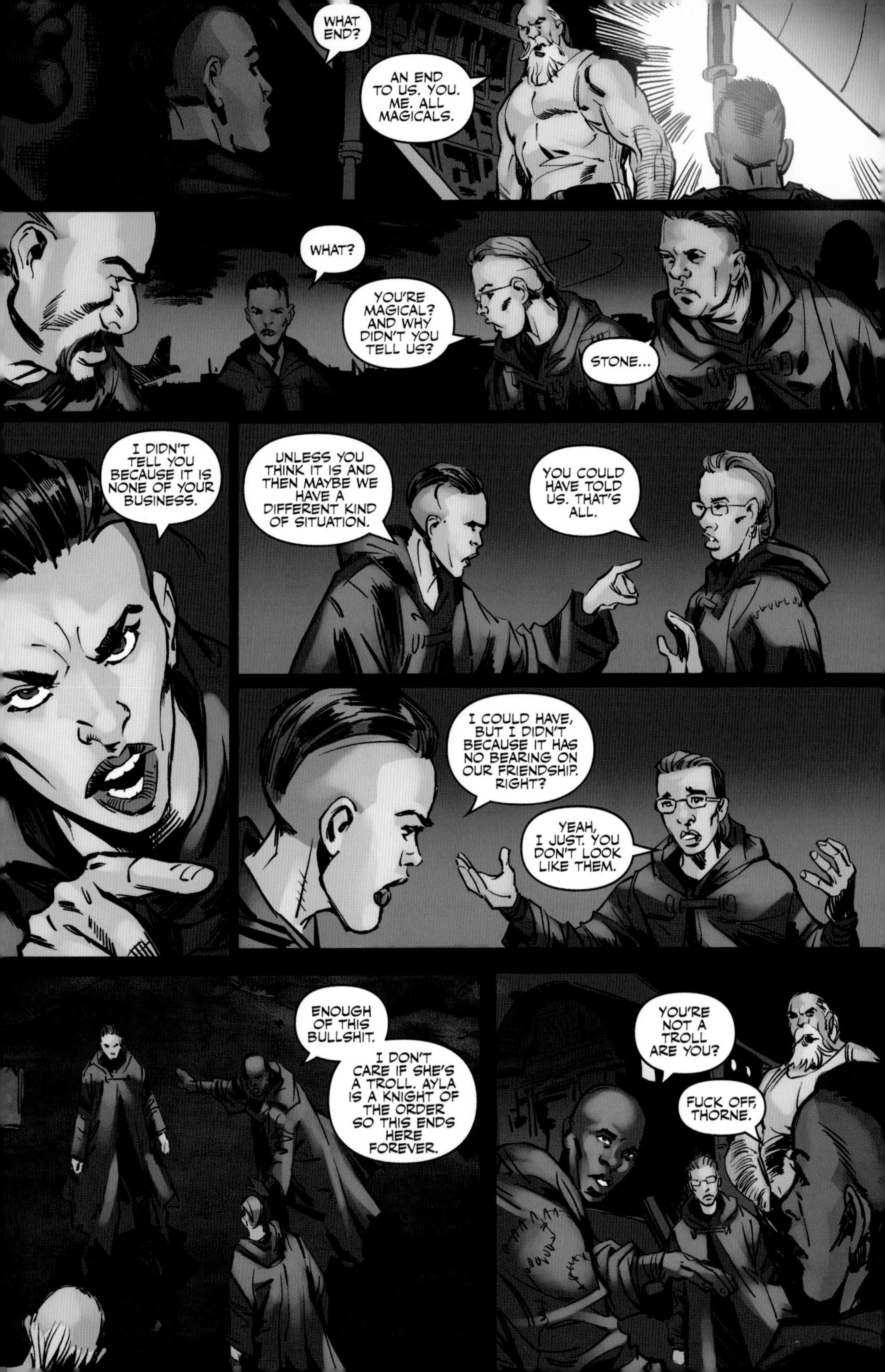
WHAT END?
AN END TO US. YOU. ME. ALL MAGICALS.
WHAT?
YOU'RE MAGICAL? AND WHY DIDN'T YOU TELL US?
STONE...
I DIDN'T TELL YOU BECAUSE IT IS NONE OF YOUR BUSINESS.
UNLESS YOU THINK IT IS AND THEN MAYBE WE HAVE A DIFFERENT KIND OF SITUATION.
YOU COULD HAVE TOLD US. THAT'S ALL.
I COULD HAVE, BUT I DIDN'T BECAUSE IT HAS NO BEARING ON OUR FRIENDSHIP. RIGHT?
YEAH, I JUST. YOU DON'T LOOK LIKE THEM.
ENOUGH OF THIS BULLSHIT.
I DON'T CARE IF SHE'S A TROLL. AYLA IS A KNIGHT OF THE ORDER SO THIS ENDS HERE FOREVER.
YOU'RE NOT A TROLL ARE YOU?
FUCK OFF, THORNE.

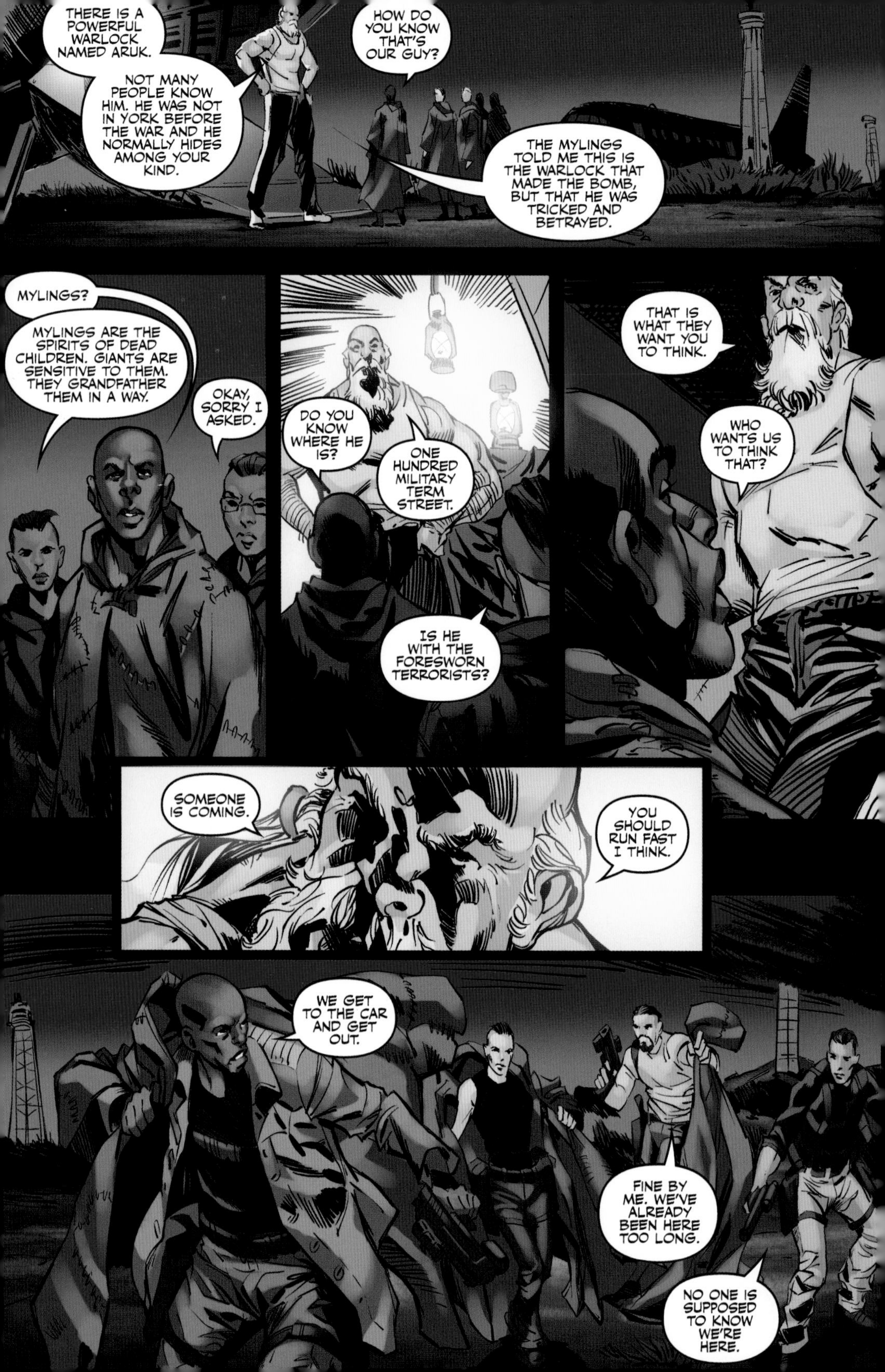
THERE IS A POWERFUL WARLOCK NAMED ARUK.
NOT MANY PEOPLE KNOW HIM. HE WAS NOT IN YORK BEFORE THE WAR AND HE NORMALLY HIDES AMONG YOUR KIND.
HOW DO YOU KNOW THAT'S OUR GUY?
THE MYLINGS TOLD ME THIS IS THE WARLOCK THAT MADE THE BOMB, BUT THAT HE WAS TRICKED AND BETRAYED.
MYLINGS?
MYLINGS ARE THE SPIRITS OF DEAD CHILDREN. GIANTS ARE SENSITIVE TO THEM. THEY GRANDFATHER THEM IN A WAY.
OKAY, SORRY I ASKED.
DO YOU KNOW WHERE HE IS?
ONE HUNDRED MILITARY TERM STREET.
IS HE WITH THE FORESWORN TERRORISTS?
THAT IS WHAT THEY WANT YOU TO THINK.
WHO WANTS US TO THINK THAT?
SOMEONE IS COMING.
YOU SHOULD RUN FAST I THINK.
WE GET TO THE CAR AND GET OUT.
FINE BY ME. WE'VE ALREADY BEEN HERE TOO LONG.
NO ONE IS SUPPOSED TO KNOW WE'RE HERE.

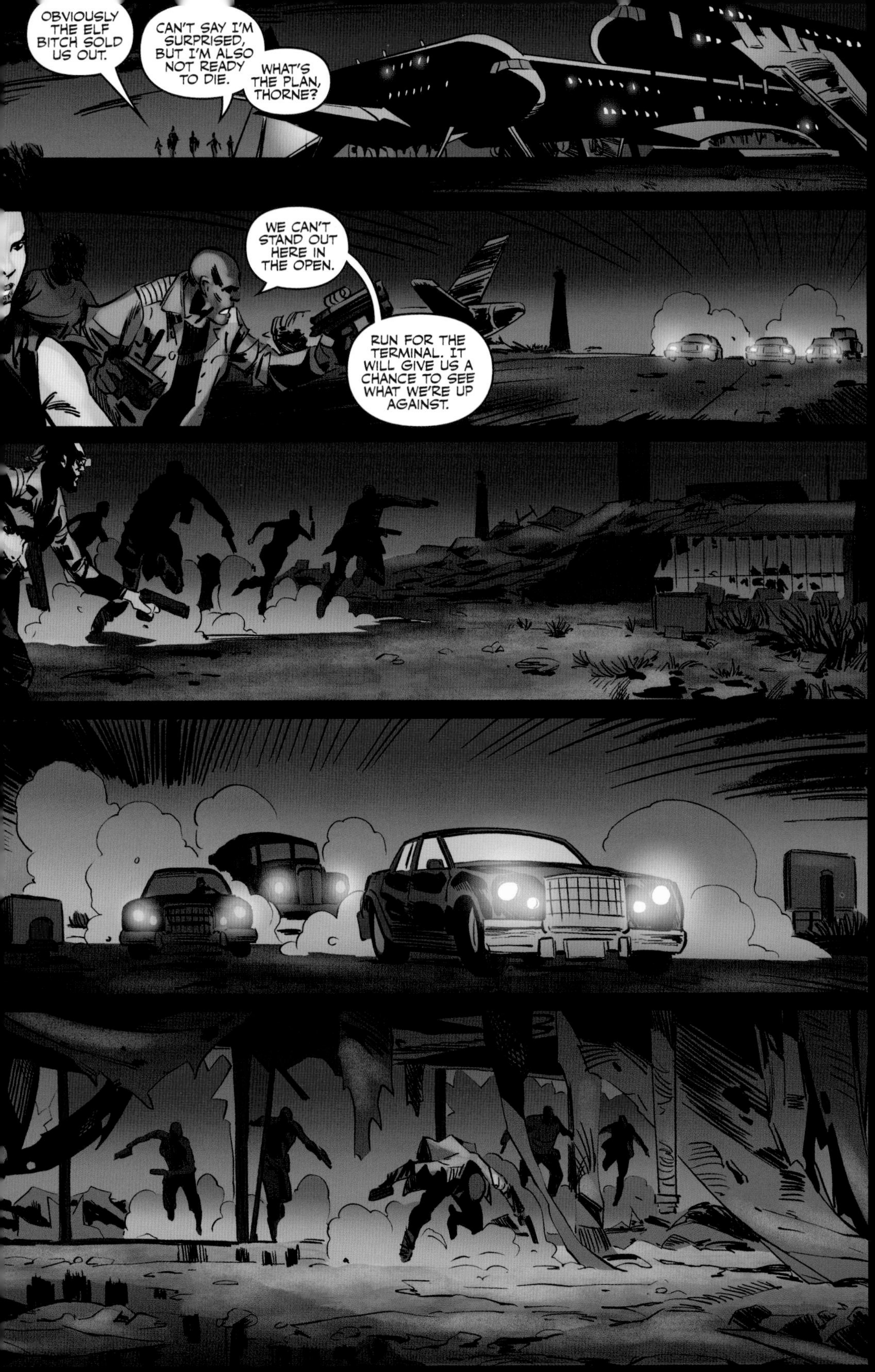
OBVIOUSLY THE ELF BITCH SOLD US OUT.
CAN'T SAY I'M SURPRISED, BUT I'M ALSO NOT READY TO DIE.
WHAT'S THE PLAN, THORNE?
WE CAN'T STAND OUT HERE IN THE OPEN.
RUN FOR THE TERMINAL. IT WILL GIVE US A CHANCE TO SEE WHAT WE'RE UP AGAINST.

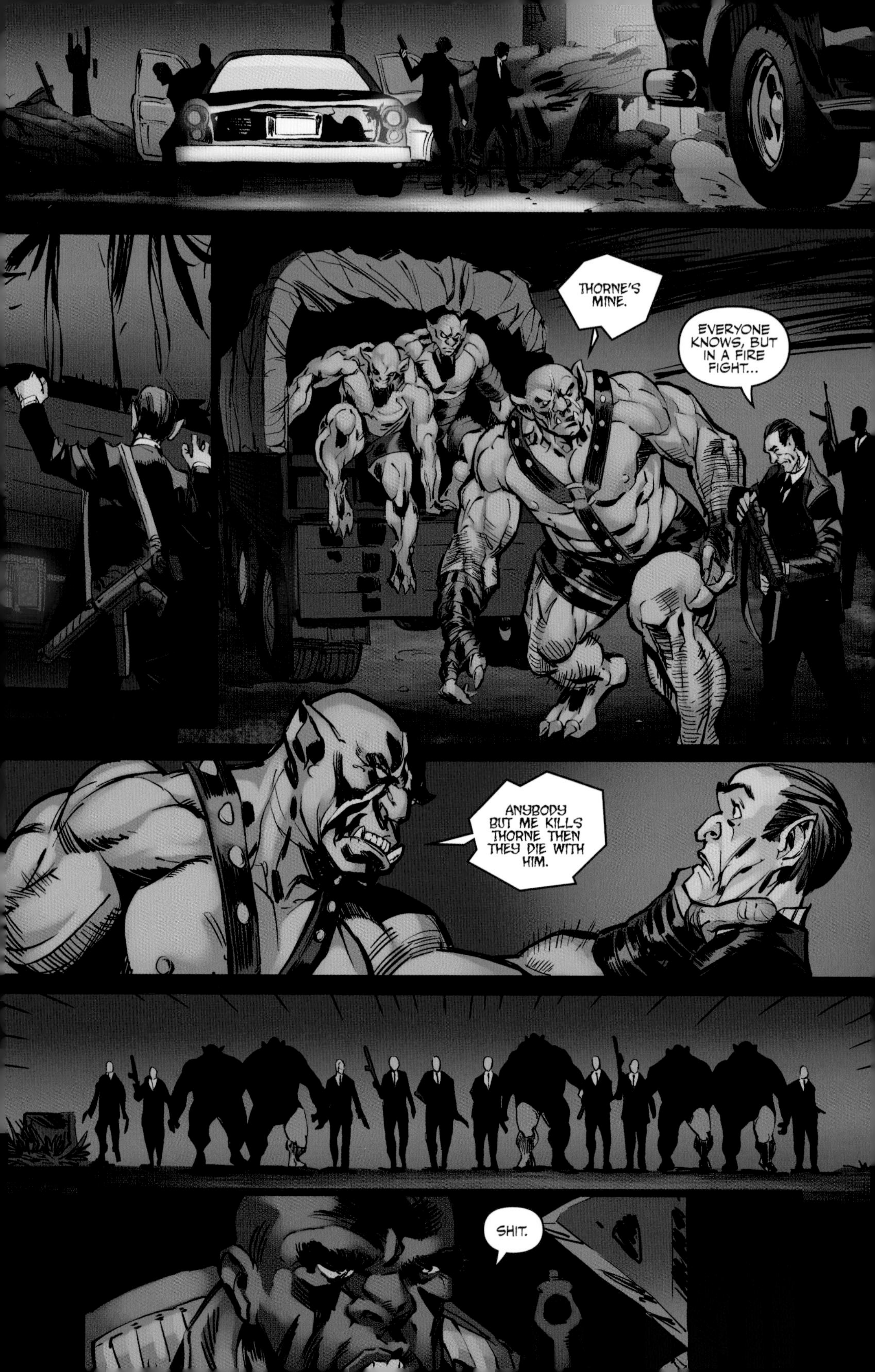
THORNE'S MINE.
EVERYONE KNOWS, BUT IN A FIRE FIGHT...
ANYBODY BUT ME KILLS THORNE THEN THEY DIE WITH HIM.
SHIT.

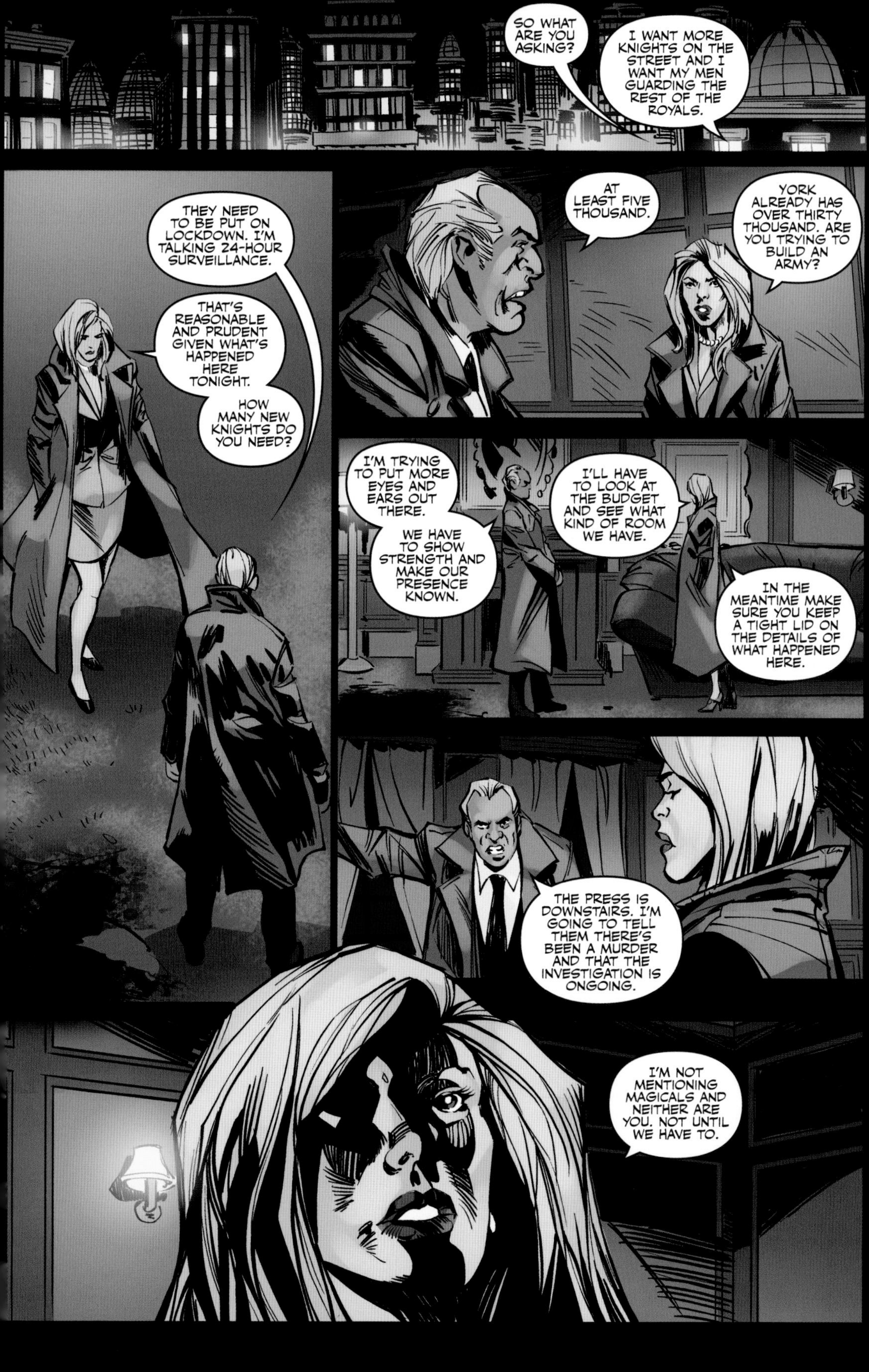
SO WHAT ARE YOU ASKING?
I WANT MORE KNIGHTS ON THE STREET AND I WANT MY MEN GUARDING THE REST OF THE ROYALS.
THEY NEED TO BE PUT ON LOCKDOWN. I'M TALKING 24-HOUR SURVEILLANCE.
THAT'S REASONABLE AND PRUDENT GIVEN WHAT'S HAPPENED HERE TONIGHT.
HOW MANY NEW KNIGHTS DO YOU NEED?
AT LEAST FIVE THOUSAND.
YORK ALREADY HAS OVER THIRTY THOUSAND. ARE YOU TRYING TO BUILD AN ARMY?
I'M TRYING TO PUT MORE EYES AND EARS OUT THERE.
WE HAVE TO SHOW STRENGTH AND MAKE OUR PRESENCE KNOWN.
I'LL HAVE TO LOOK AT THE BUDGET AND SEE WHAT KIND OF ROOM WE HAVE.
IN THE MEANTIME MAKE SURE YOU KEEP A TIGHT LID ON THE DETAILS OF WHAT HAPPENED HERE.
THE PRESS IS DOWNSTAIRS. I'M GOING TO TELL THEM THERE'S BEEN A MURDER AND THAT THE INVESTIGATION IS ONGOING.
I'M NOT MENTIONING MAGICALS AND NEITHER ARE YOU. NOT UNTIL WE HAVE TO.

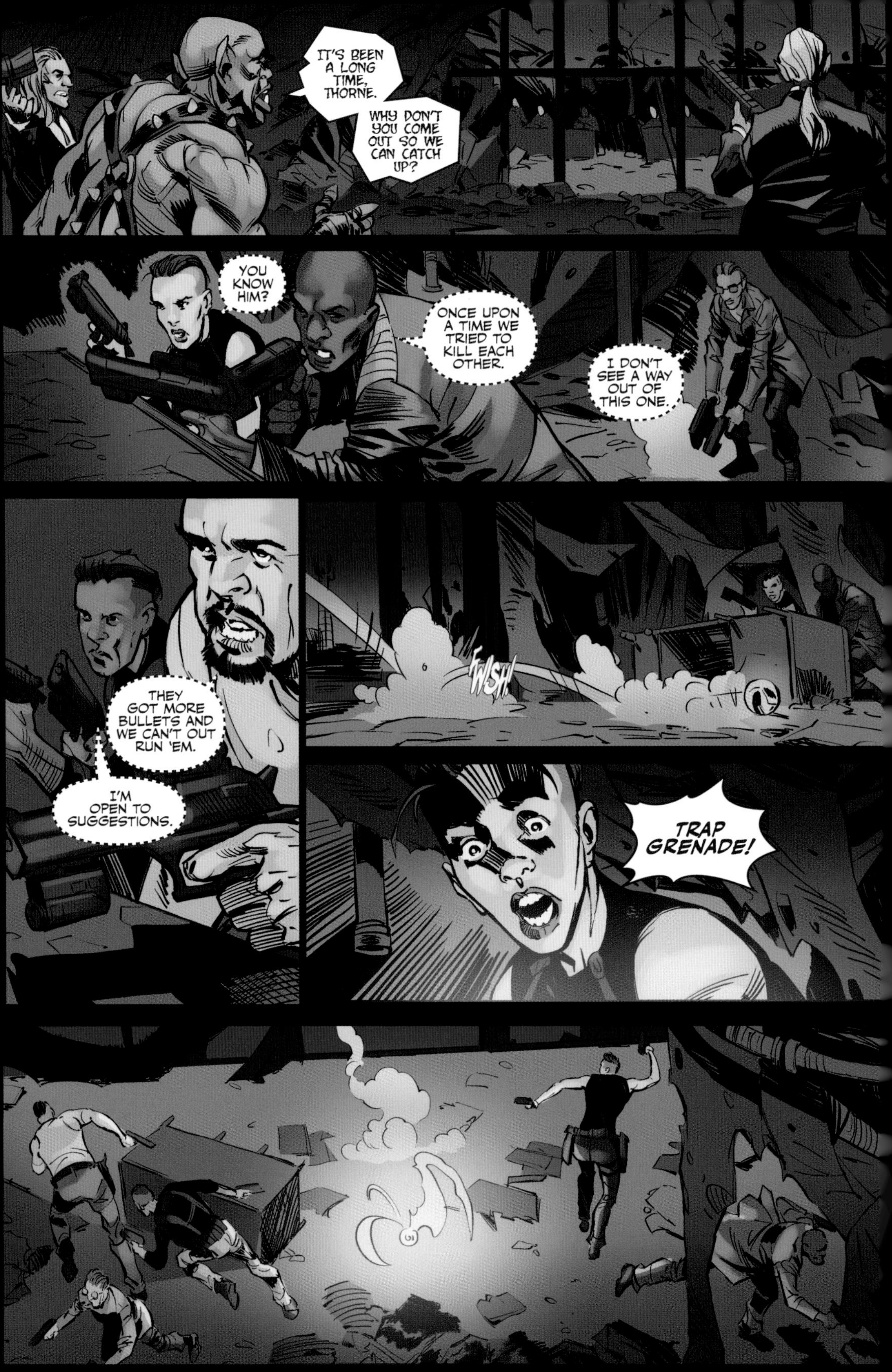
IT'S BEEN A LONG TIME, THORNE.
WHY DON'T YOU COME OUT SO WE CAN CATCH UP?
YOU KNOW HIM?
ONCE UPON A TIME WE TRIED TO KILL EACH OTHER.
I DON'T SEE A WAY OUT OF THIS ONE.
THEY GOT MORE BULLETS AND WE CAN'T OUT RUN 'EM.
I'M OPEN TO SUGGESTIONS.
FWSH!
TRAP GRENADE!

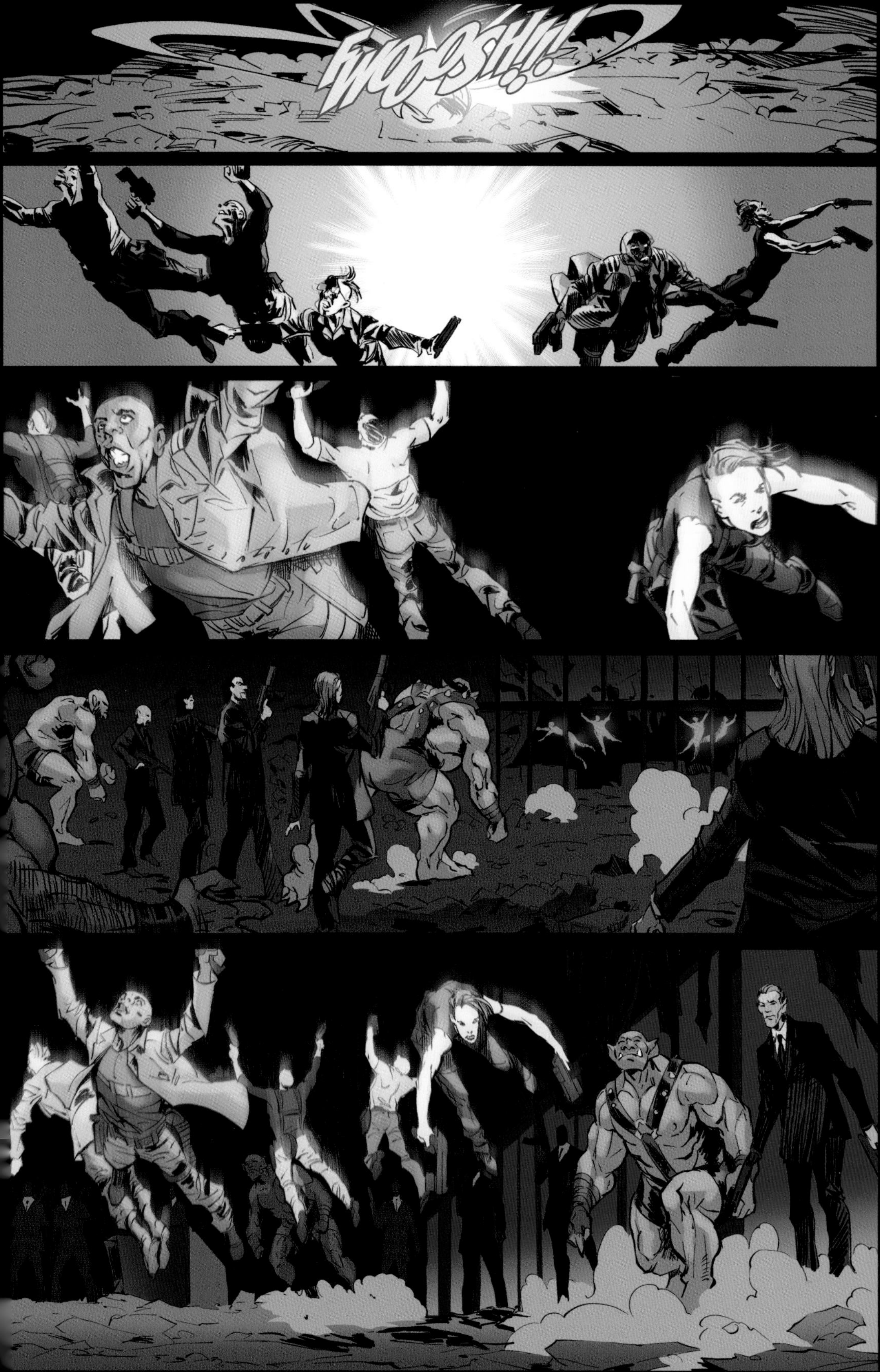
FWOOOOSHH!!

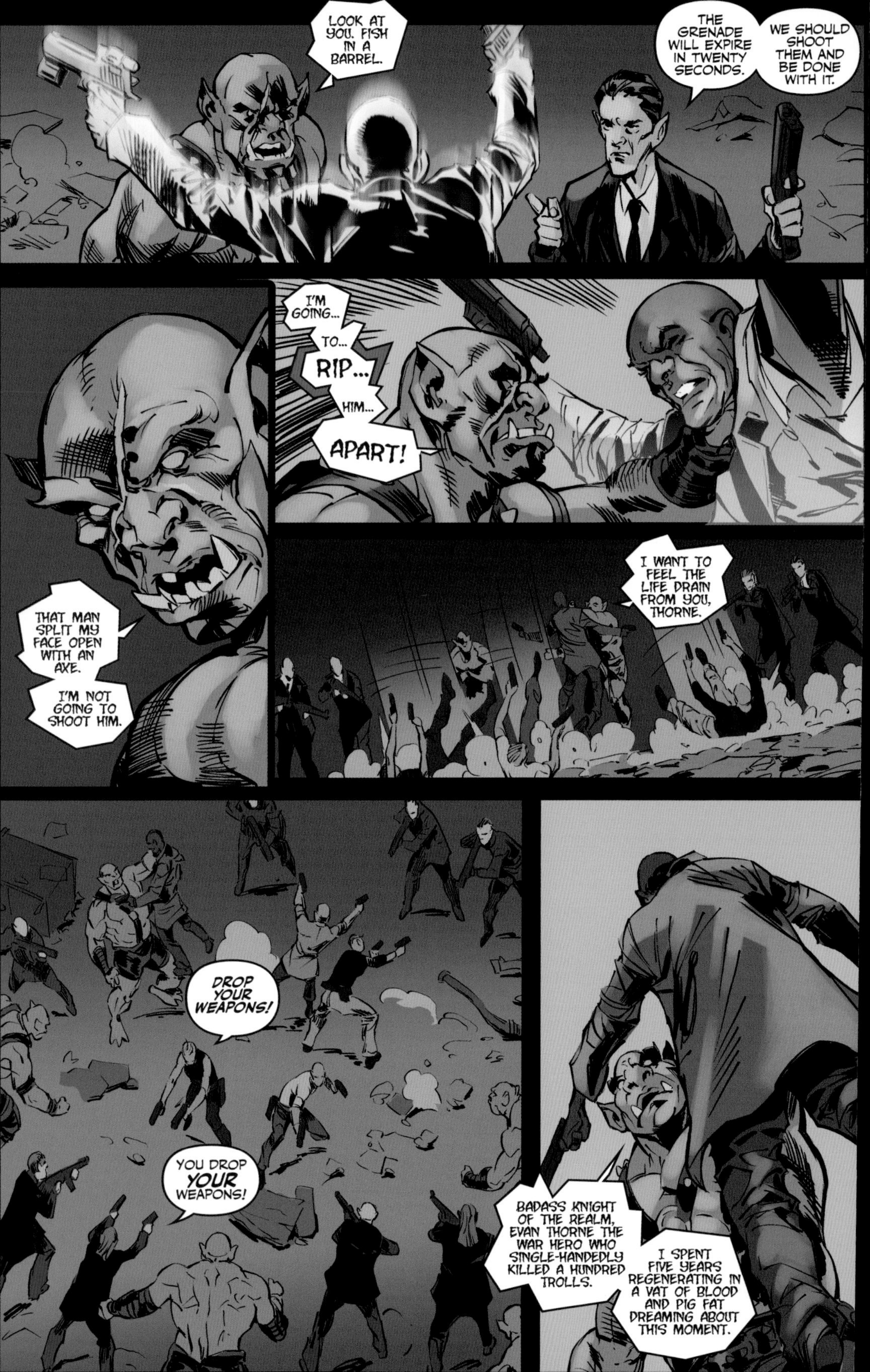
LOOK AT YOU. FISH IN A BARREL.
THE GRENADE WILL EXPIRE IN TWENTY SECONDS.
WE SHOULD SHOOT THEM AND BE DONE WITH IT.
THAT MAN SPLIT MY FACE OPEN WITH AN AXE.
I'M NOT GOING TO SHOOT HIM.
I'M GOING...
TO...
RIP...
HIM...
APART!
I WANT TO FEEL THE LIFE DRAIN FROM YOU, THORNE.
DROP YOUR WEAPONS!
YOU DROP YOUR WEAPONS!
BADASS KNIGHT OF THE REALM, EVAN THORNE THE WAR HERO WHO SINGLE-HANDEDLY KILLED A HUNDRED TROLLS.
I SPENT FIVE YEARS REGENERATING IN A VAT OF BLOOD AND PIG FAT DREAMING ABOUT THIS MOMENT.

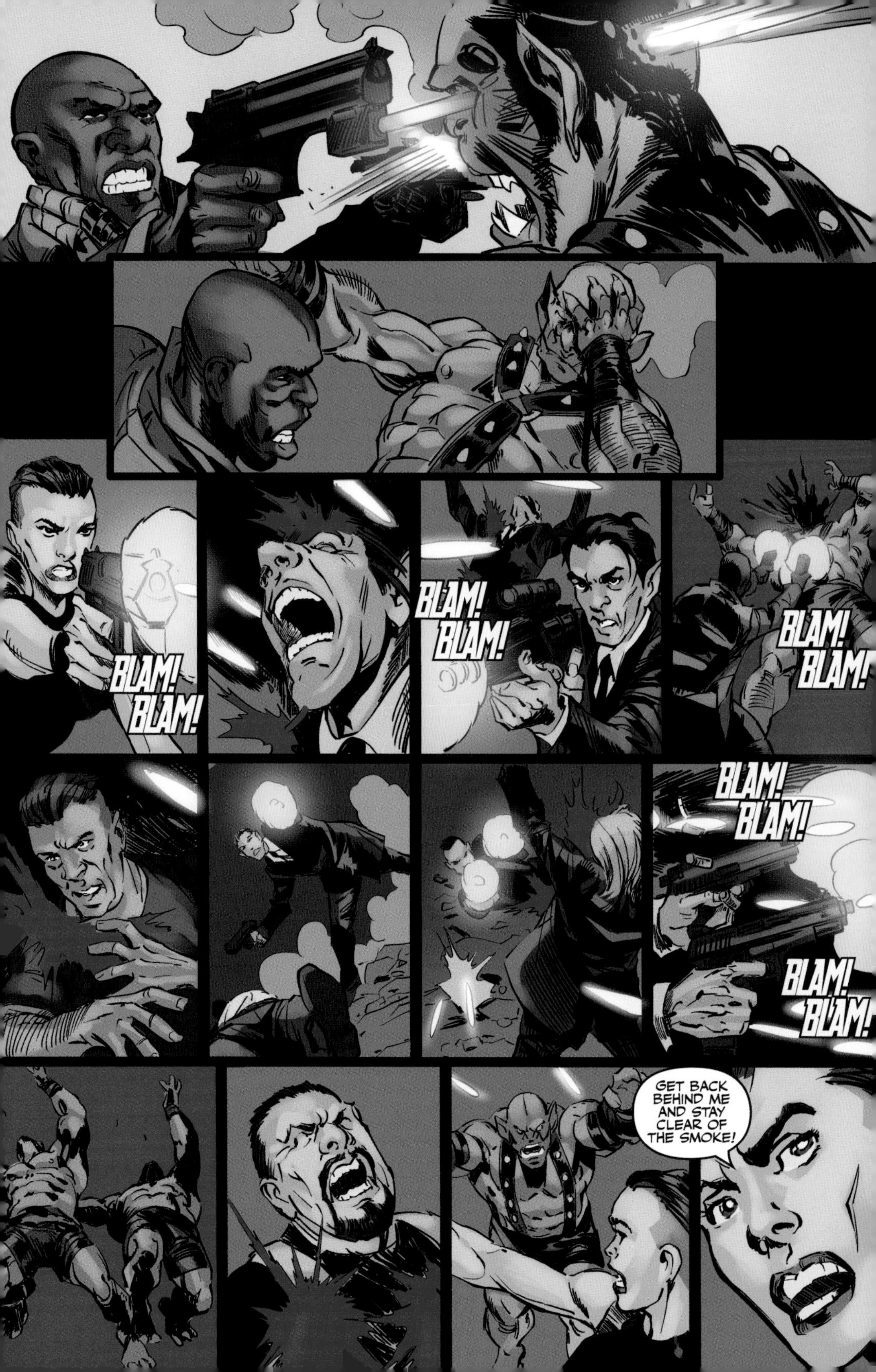
BLAM! BLAM!
BLAM! BLAM!
BLAM! BLAM!
BLAM! BLAM!
BLAM! BLAM!
GET BACK BEHIND ME AND STAY CLEAR OF THE SMOKE!

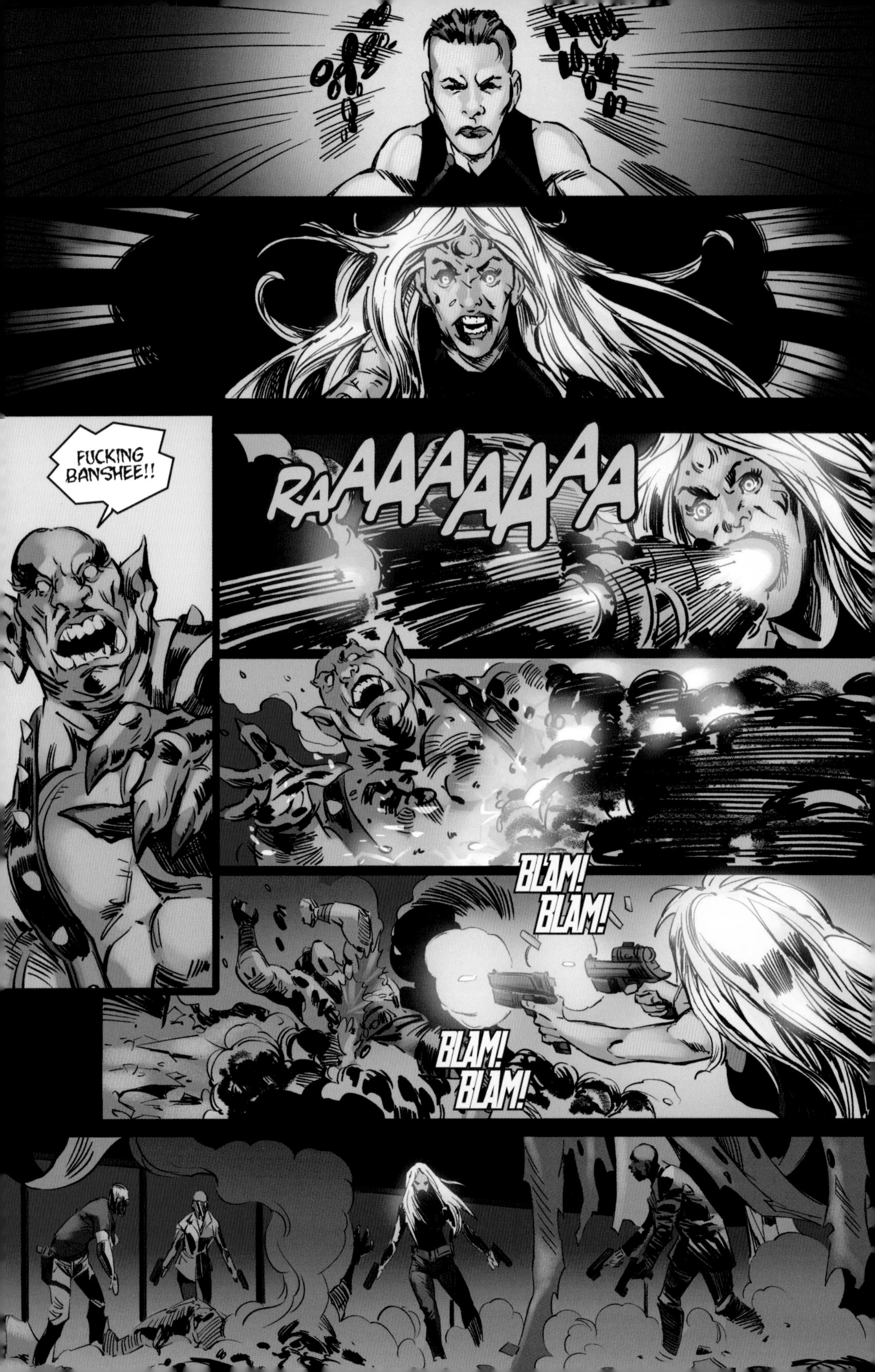
FUCKING BANSHEE!!
RAAAAAAAA
BLAM! BLAM!
BLAM! BLAM!

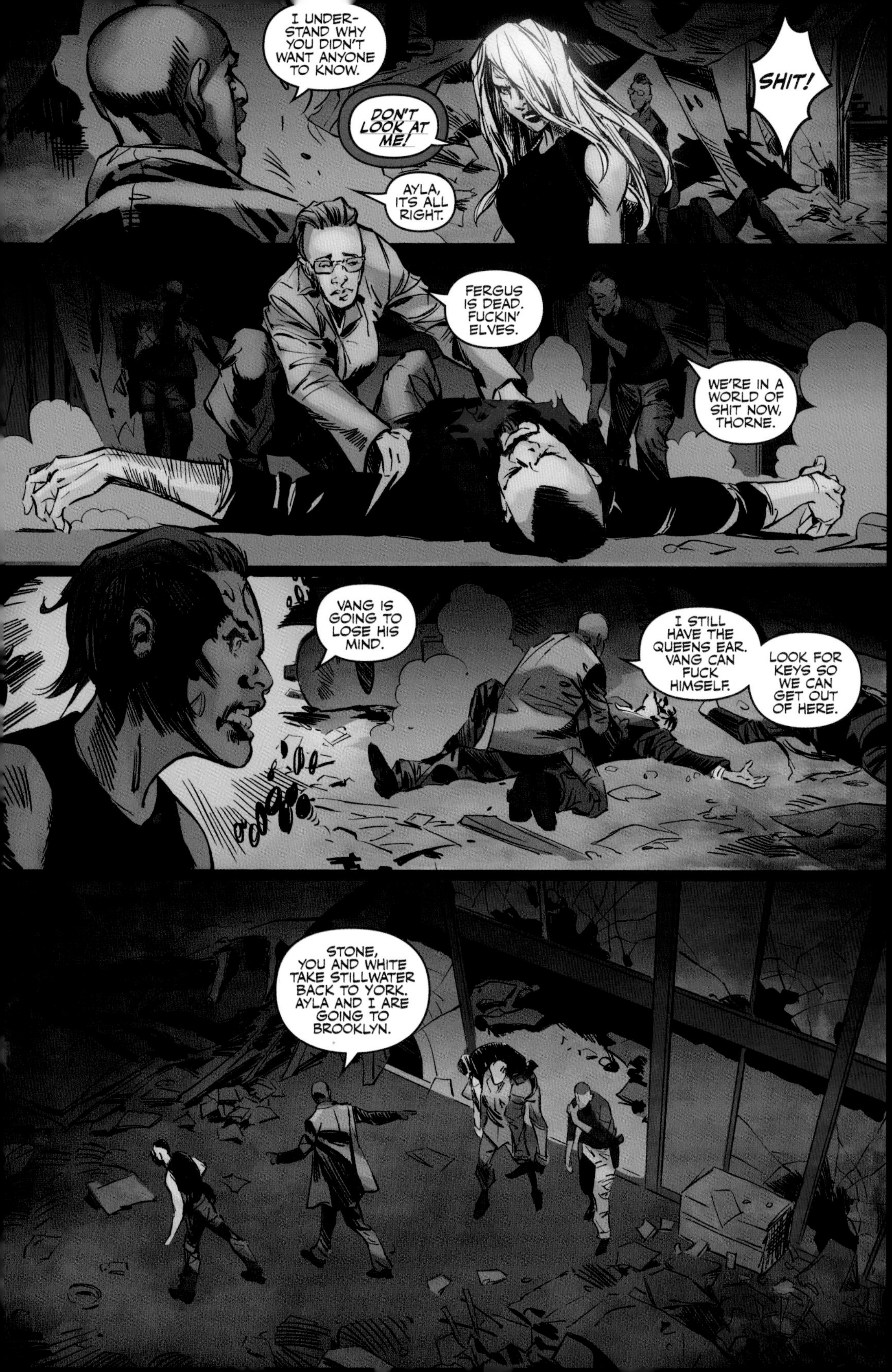
I UNDER-STAND WHY YOU DIDN'T WANT ANYONE TO KNOW.
DON'T LOOK AT ME!
SHIT!
AYLA, IT'S ALL RIGHT.
FERGUS IS DEAD. FUCKIN' ELVES.
WE'RE IN A WORLD OF SHIT NOW, THORNE.
VANG IS GOING TO LOSE HIS MIND.
I STILL HAVE THE QUEENS EAR. VANG CAN FUCK HIMSELF.
LOOK FOR KEYS SO WE CAN GET OUT OF HERE.
STONE, YOU AND WHITE TAKE STILLWATER BACK TO YORK. AYLA AND I ARE GOING TO BROOKLYN.

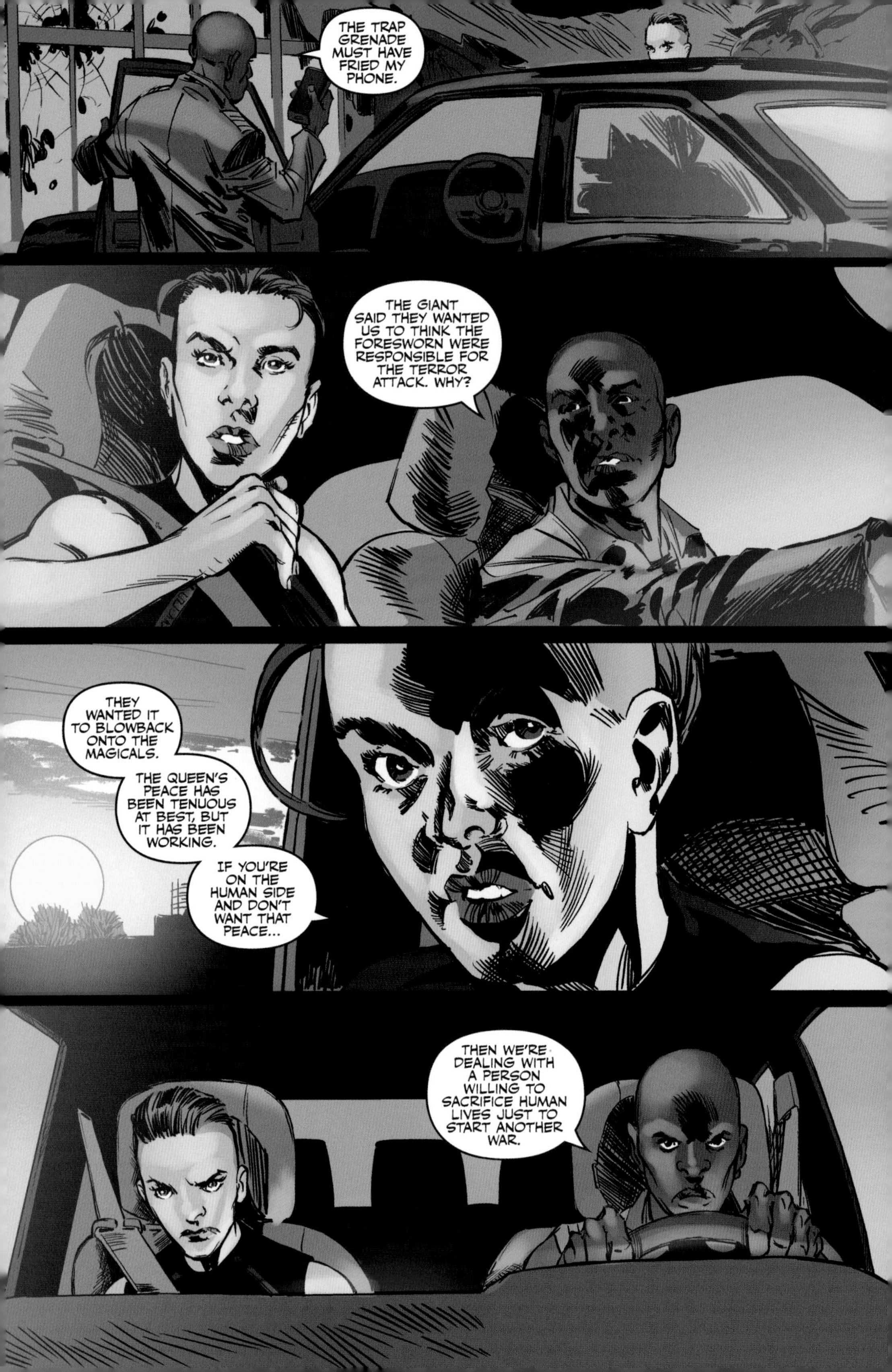
THE TRAP GRENADE MUST HAVE FRIED MY PHONE.
THE GIANT SAID THEY WANTED US TO THINK THE FORESWORN WERE RESPONSIBLE FOR THE TERROR ATTACK. WHY?
THEY WANTED IT TO BLOWBACK ONTO THE MAGICALS.
THE QUEEN'S PEACE HAS BEEN TENUOUS AT BEST, BUT IT HAS BEEN WORKING.
IF YOU'RE ON THE HUMAN SIDE AND DON'T WANT THAT PEACE...
THEN WE'RE DEALING WITH A PERSON WILLING TO SACRIFICE HUMAN LIVES JUST TO START ANOTHER WAR.

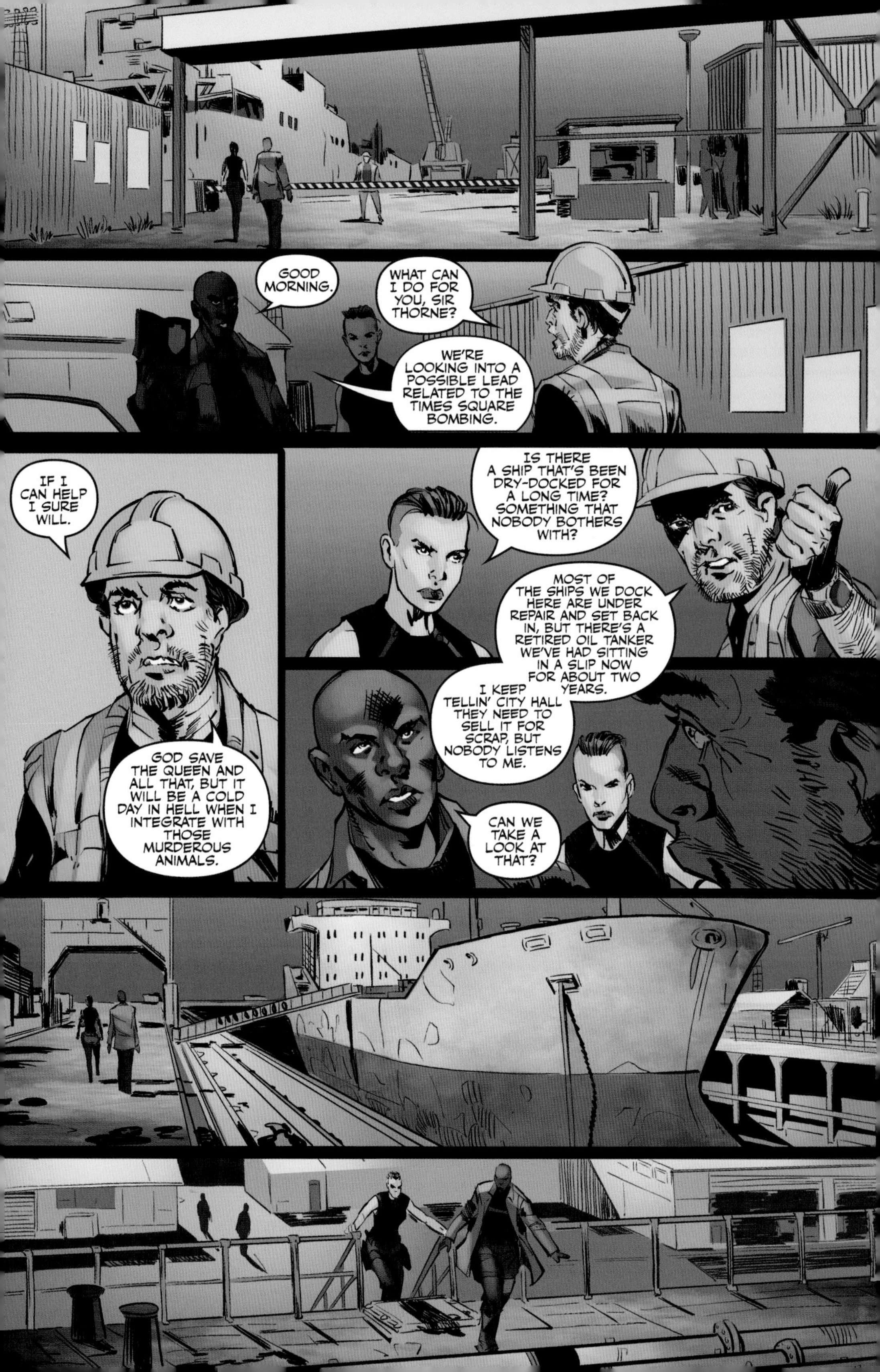
GOOD MORNING.
WHAT CAN I DO FOR YOU, SIR THORNE?
WE'RE LOOKING INTO A POSSIBLE LEAD RELATED TO THE TIMES SQUARE BOMBING.
IF I CAN HELP I SURE WILL.
GOD SAVE THE QUEEN AND ALL THAT, BUT IT WILL BE A COLD DAY IN HELL WHEN I INTEGRATE WITH THOSE MURDEROUS ANIMALS.
IS THERE A SHIP THAT'S BEEN DRY-DOCKED FOR A LONG TIME? SOMETHING THAT NOBODY BOTHERS WITH?
MOST OF THE SHIPS WE DOCK HERE ARE UNDER REPAIR AND SET BACK IN, BUT THERE'S A RETIRED OIL TANKER WE'VE HAD SITTING IN A SLIP NOW FOR ABOUT TWO YEARS.
I KEEP TELLIN' CITY HALL THEY NEED TO SELL IT FOR SCRAP, BUT NOBODY LISTENS TO ME.
CAN WE TAKE A LOOK AT THAT?

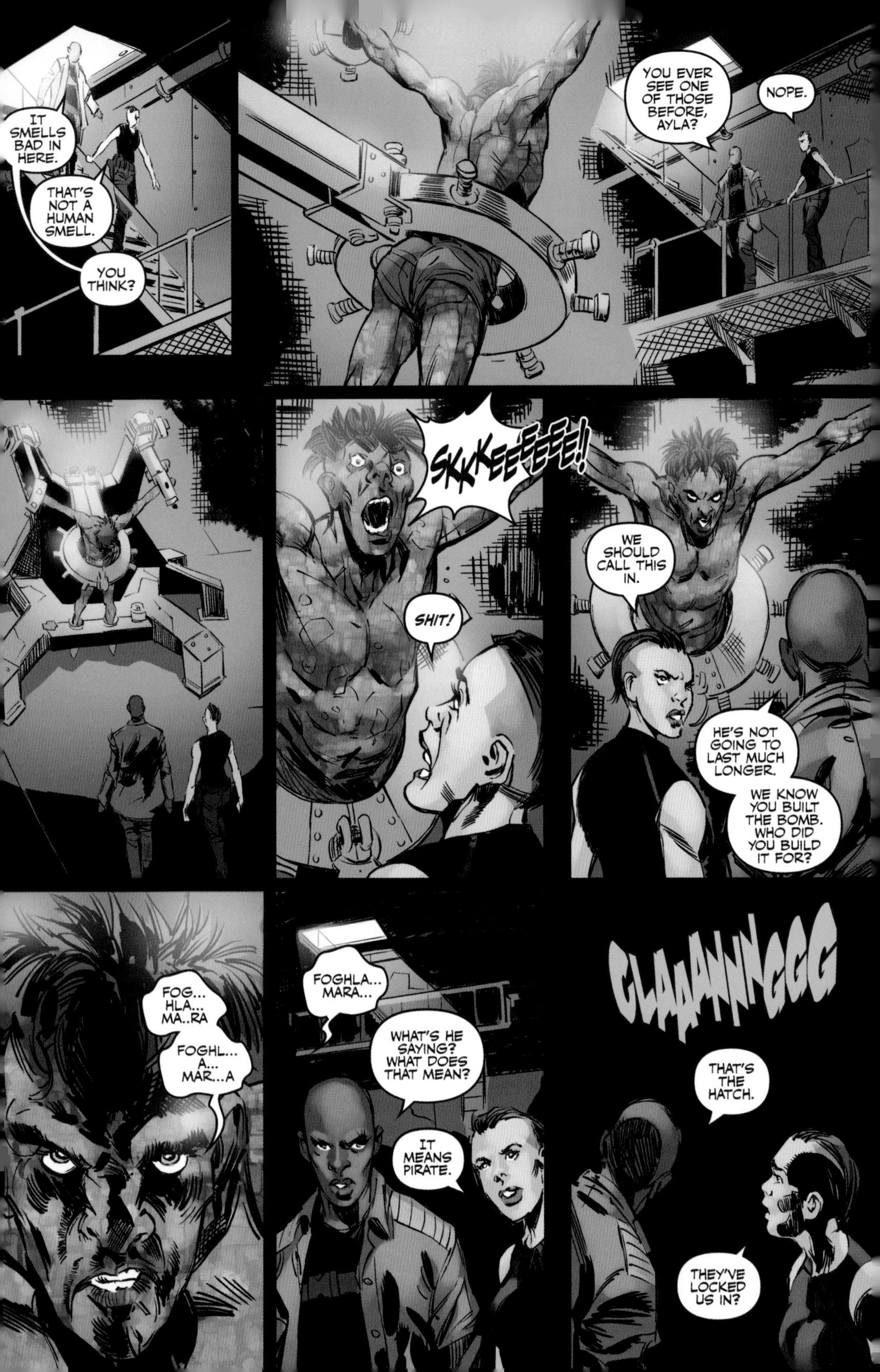
IT SMELLS BAD IN HERE.
THAT'S NOT A HUMAN SMELL.
YOU THINK?
YOU EVER SEE ONE OF THOSE BEFORE, AYLA?
NOPE.
SKKKEEEEEEE!
SHIT!
WE SHOULD CALL THIS IN.
HE'S NOT GOING TO LAST MUCH LONGER.
WE KNOW YOU BUILT THE BOMB. WHO DID YOU BUILD IT FOR?
FOG... HLA... MA..RA
FOGHL... A... MAR...A
FOGHLA... MARA...
WHAT'S HE SAYING? WHAT DOES THAT MEAN?
IT MEANS PIRATE.
CLAAANNGGG
THAT'S THE HATCH.
THEY'VE LOCKED US IN?

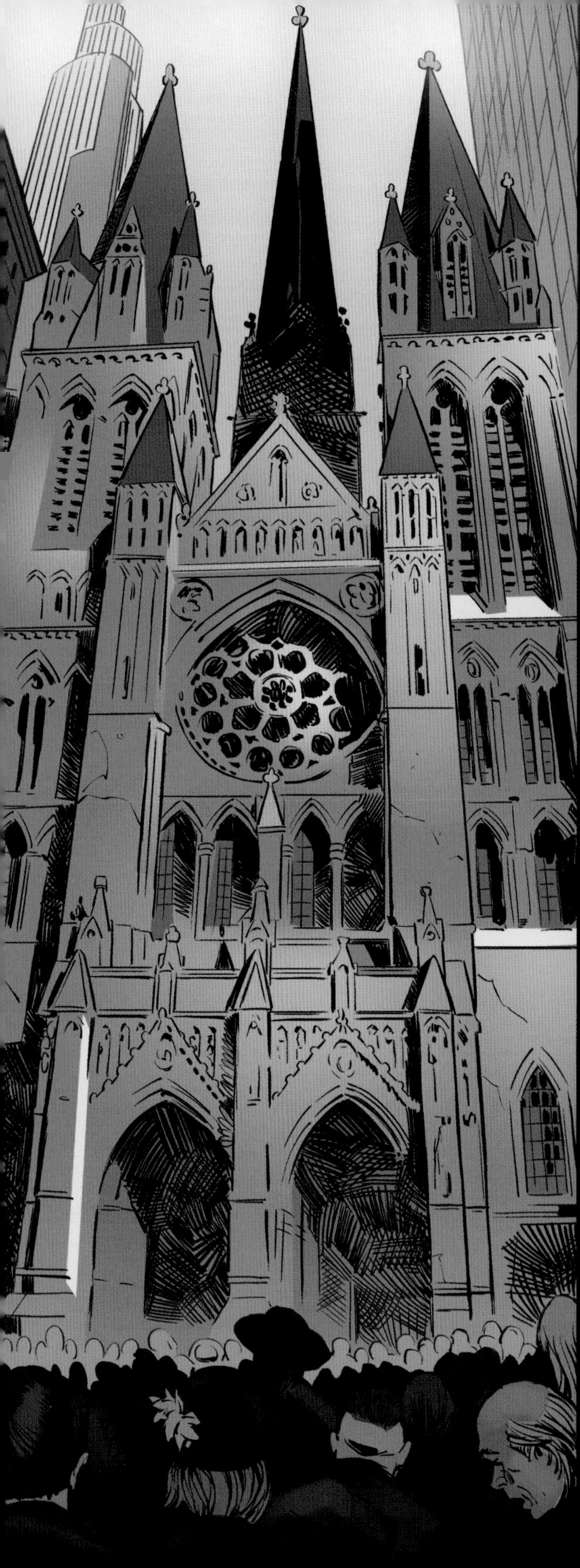

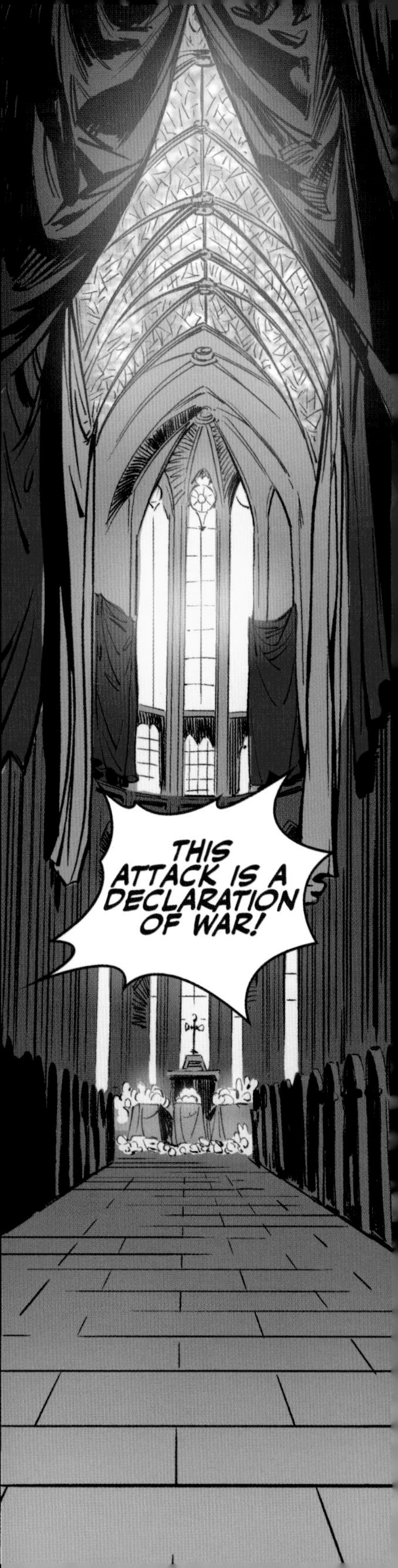
THIS ATTACK IS A DECLARATION OF WAR!

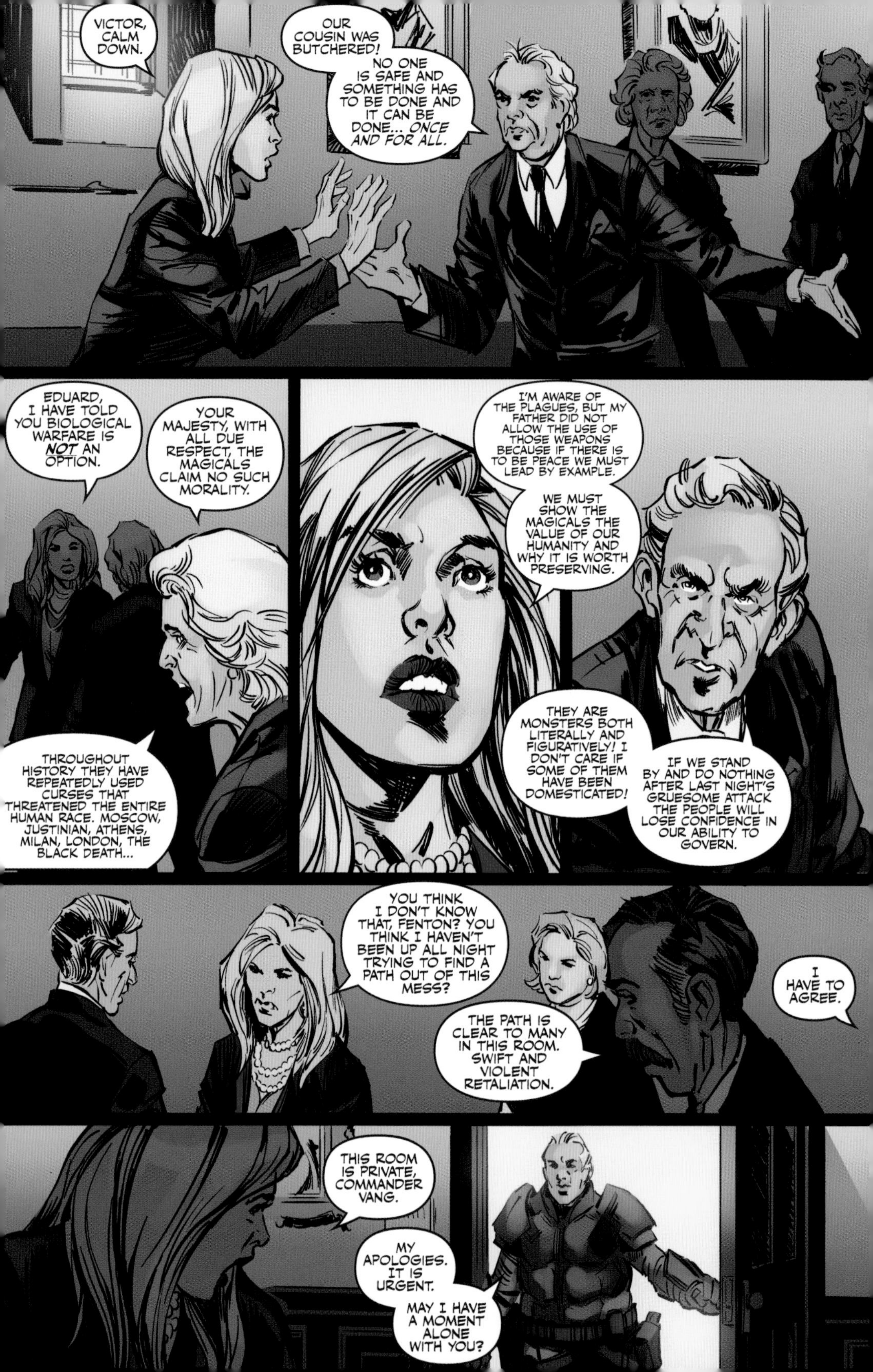
VICTOR, CALM DOWN.
OUR COUSIN WAS BUTCHERED!
NO ONE IS SAFE AND SOMETHING HAS TO BE DONE AND IT CAN BE DONE... ONCE AND FOR ALL.
EDUARD, I HAVE TOLD YOU BIOLOGICAL WARFARE IS NOT AN OPTION.
YOUR MAJESTY, WITH ALL DUE RESPECT, THE MAGICALS CLAIM NO SUCH MORALITY.
THROUGHOUT HISTORY THEY HAVE REPEATEDLY USED CURSES THAT THREATENED THE ENTIRE HUMAN RACE. MOSCOW, JUSTINIAN, ATHENS, MILAN, LONDON, THE BLACK DEATH...
I'M AWARE OF THE PLAGUES, BUT MY FATHER DID NOT ALLOW THE USE OF THOSE WEAPONS BECAUSE IF THERE IS TO BE PEACE WE MUST LEAD BY EXAMPLE.
WE MUST SHOW THE MAGICALS THE VALUE OF OUR HUMANITY AND WHY IT IS WORTH PRESERVING.
THEY ARE MONSTERS BOTH LITERALLY AND FIGURATIVELY! I DON'T CARE IF SOME OF THEM HAVE BEEN DOMESTICATED!
IF WE STAND BY AND DO NOTHING AFTER LAST NIGHT'S GRUESOME ATTACK THE PEOPLE WILL LOSE CONFIDENCE IN OUR ABILITY TO GOVERN.
YOU THINK I DON'T KNOW THAT, FENTON? YOU THINK I HAVEN'T BEEN UP ALL NIGHT TRYING TO FIND A PATH OUT OF THIS MESS?
THE PATH IS CLEAR TO MANY IN THIS ROOM. SWIFT AND VIOLENT RETALIATION.
I HAVE TO AGREE.
THIS ROOM IS PRIVATE, COMMANDER VANG.
MY APOLOGIES. IT IS URGENT.
MAY I HAVE A MOMENT ALONE WITH YOU?

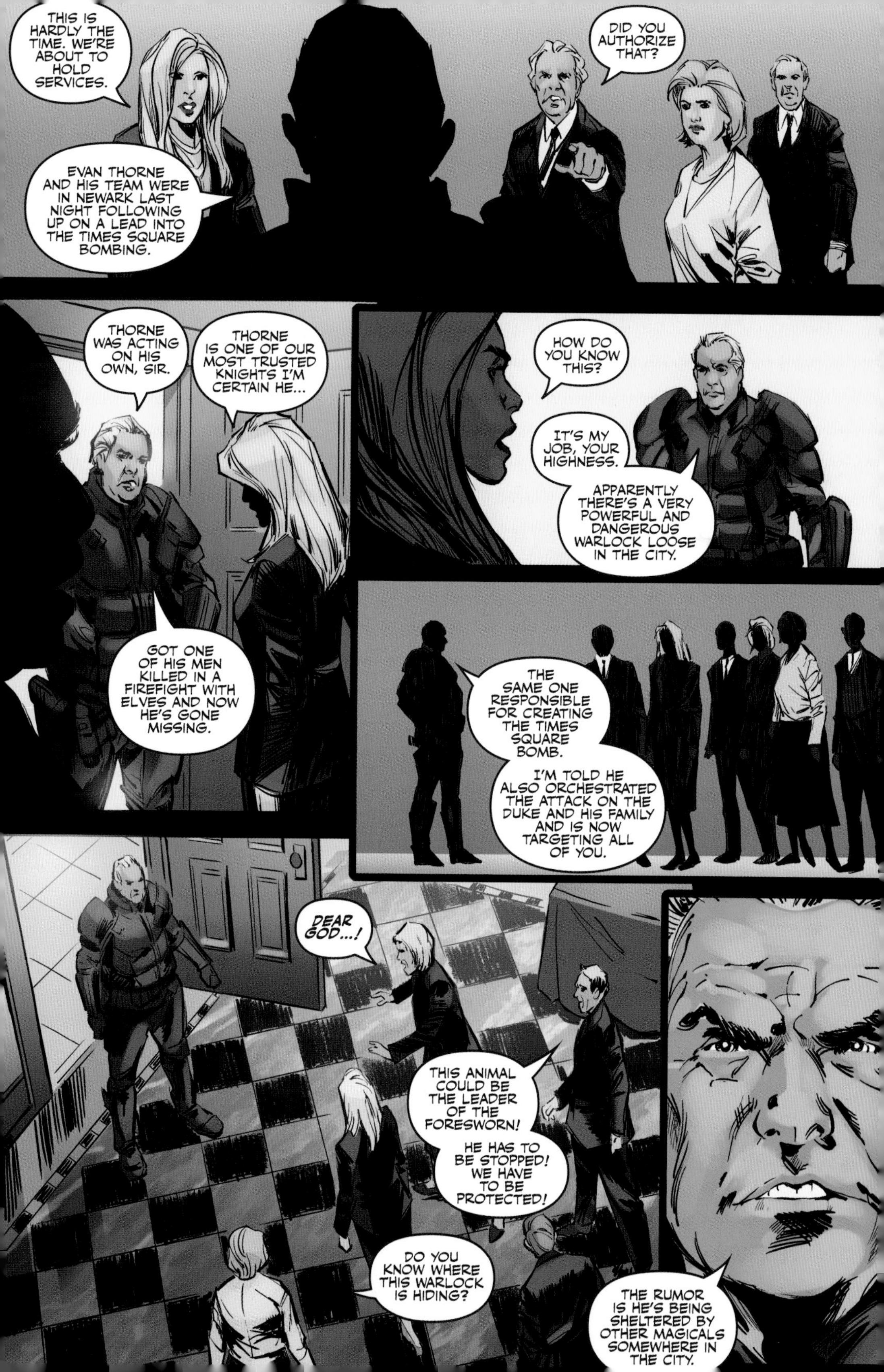
THIS IS HARDLY THE TIME. WE'RE ABOUT TO HOLD SERVICES.
EVAN THORNE AND HIS TEAM WERE IN NEWARK LAST NIGHT FOLLOWING UP ON A LEAD INTO THE TIMES SQUARE BOMBING.
DID YOU AUTHORIZE THAT?
THORNE WAS ACTING ON HIS OWN, SIR.
THORNE IS ONE OF OUR MOST TRUSTED KNIGHTS I'M CERTAIN HE...
GOT ONE OF HIS MEN KILLED IN A FIREFIGHT WITH ELVES AND NOW HE'S GONE MISSING.
HOW DO YOU KNOW THIS?
IT'S MY JOB, YOUR HIGHNESS.
APPARENTLY THERE'S A VERY POWERFUL AND DANGEROUS WARLOCK LOOSE IN THE CITY.
THE SAME ONE RESPONSIBLE FOR CREATING THE TIMES SQUARE BOMB.
I'M TOLD HE ALSO ORCHESTRATED THE ATTACK ON THE DUKE AND HIS FAMILY AND IS NOW TARGETING ALL OF YOU.
DEAR GOD...!
THIS ANIMAL COULD BE THE LEADER OF THE FORESWORN!
HE HAS TO BE STOPPED! WE HAVE TO BE PROTECTED!
DO YOU KNOW WHERE THIS WARLOCK IS HIDING?
THE RUMOR IS HE'S BEING SHELTERED BY OTHER MAGICALS SOMEWHERE IN THE CITY.

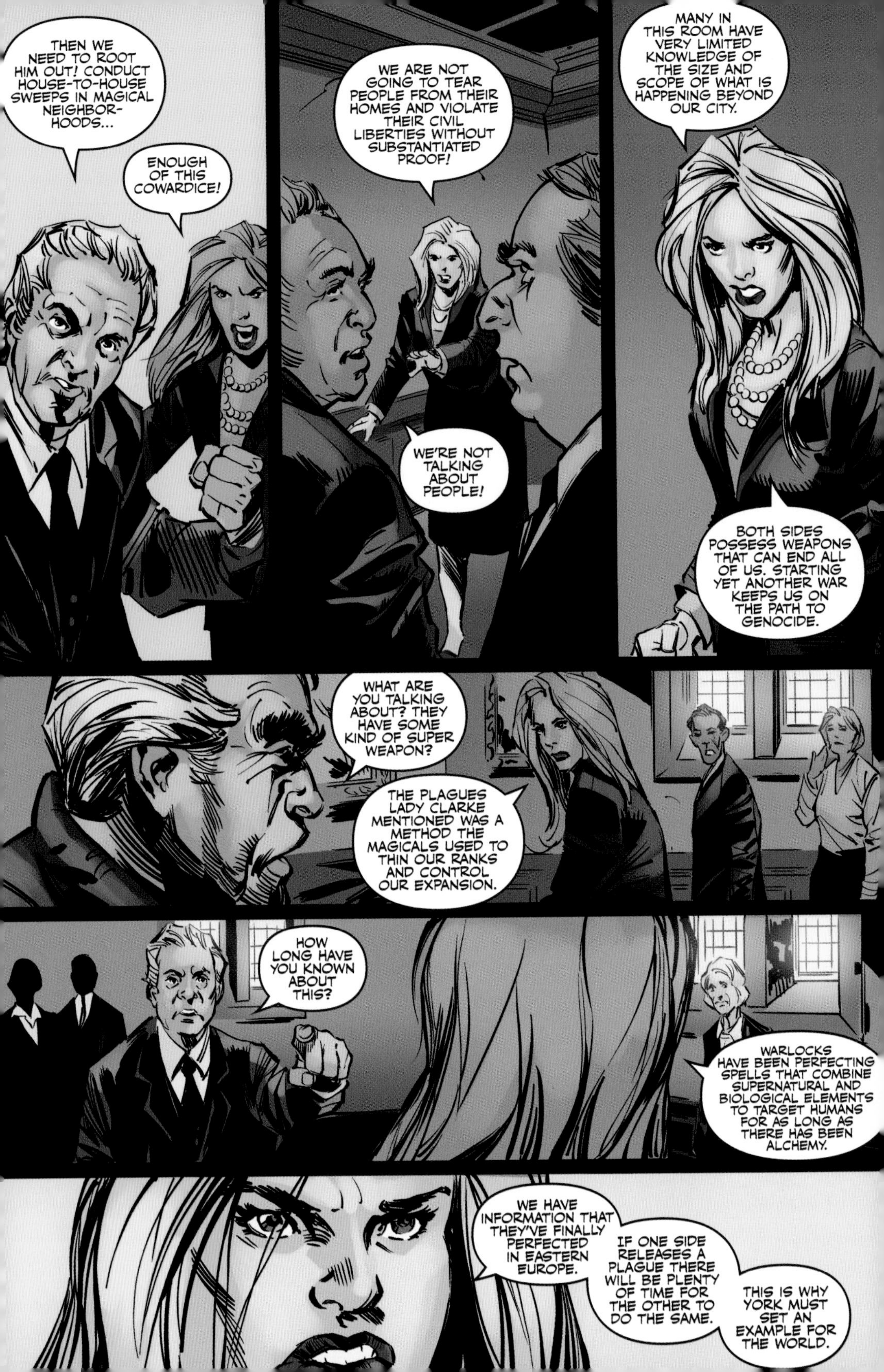
THEN WE NEED TO ROOT HIM OUT! CONDUCT HOUSE-TO-HOUSE SWEEPS IN MAGICAL NEIGHBOR-HOODS...
ENOUGH OF THIS COWARDICE!
WE ARE NOT GOING TO TEAR PEOPLE FROM THEIR HOMES AND VIOLATE THEIR CIVIL LIBERTIES WITHOUT SUBSTANTIATED PROOF!
WE'RE NOT TALKING ABOUT PEOPLE!
MANY IN THIS ROOM HAVE VERY LIMITED KNOWLEDGE OF THE SIZE AND SCOPE OF WHAT IS HAPPENING BEYOND OUR CITY.
BOTH SIDES POSSESS WEAPONS THAT CAN END ALL OF US. STARTING YET ANOTHER WAR KEEPS US ON THE PATH TO GENOCIDE.
WHAT ARE YOU TALKING ABOUT? THEY HAVE SOME KIND OF SUPER WEAPON?
THE PLAGUES LADY CLARKE MENTIONED WAS A METHOD THE MAGICALS USED TO THIN OUR RANKS AND CONTROL OUR EXPANSION.
HOW LONG HAVE YOU KNOWN ABOUT THIS?
WARLOCKS HAVE BEEN PERFECTING SPELLS THAT COMBINE SUPERNATURAL AND BIOLOGICAL ELEMENTS TO TARGET HUMANS FOR AS LONG AS THERE HAS BEEN ALCHEMY.
WE HAVE INFORMATION THAT THEY'VE FINALLY PERFECTED IN EASTERN EUROPE.
IF ONE SIDE RELEASES A PLAGUE THERE WILL BE PLENTY OF TIME FOR THE OTHER TO DO THE SAME.
THIS IS WHY YORK MUST SET AN EXAMPLE FOR THE WORLD.

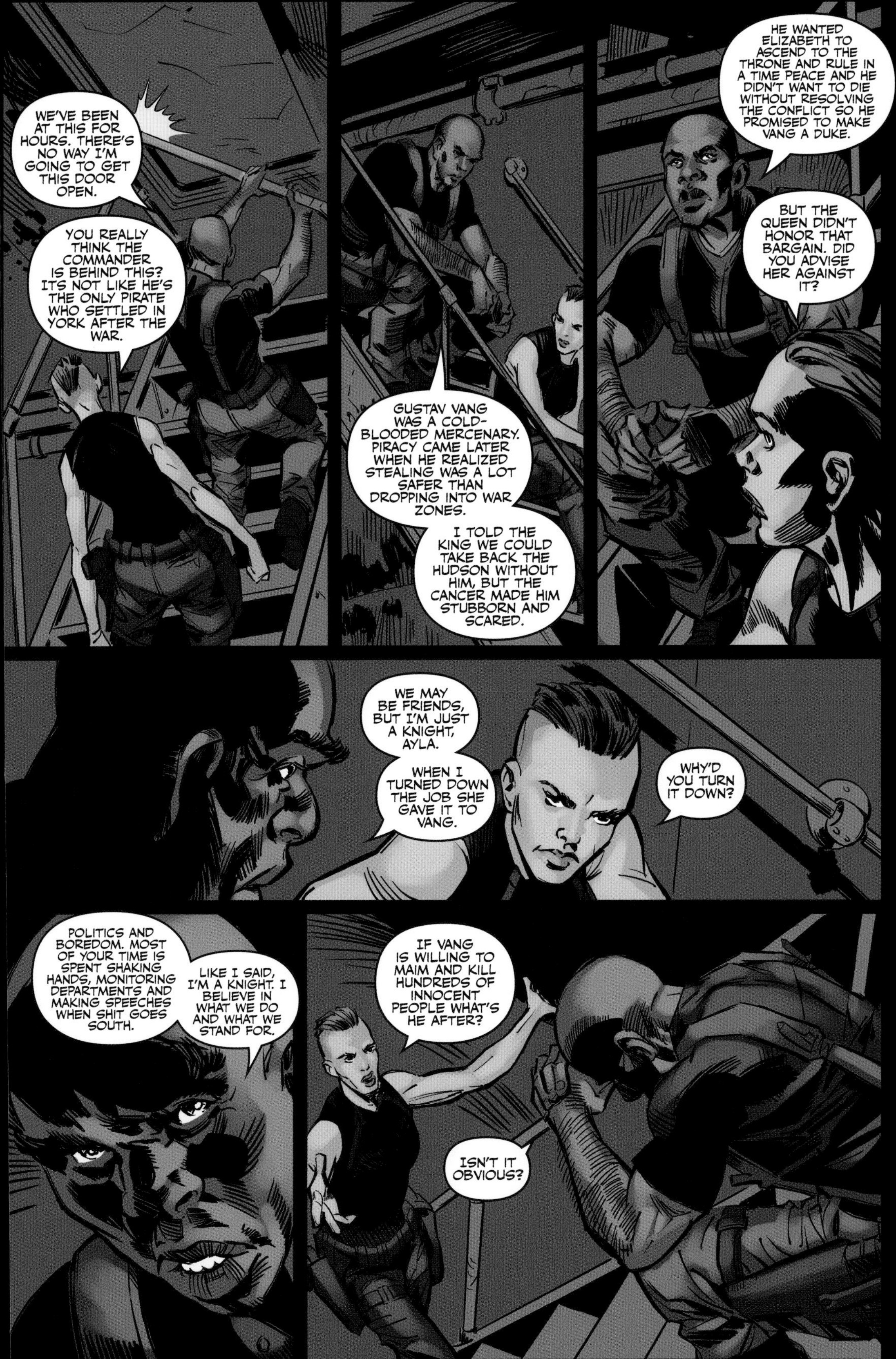
WE'VE BEEN AT THIS FOR HOURS. THERE'S NO WAY I'M GOING TO GET THIS DOOR OPEN.
YOU REALLY THINK THE COMMANDER IS BEHIND THIS? ITS NOT LIKE HE'S THE ONLY PIRATE WHO SETTLED IN YORK AFTER THE WAR.
GUSTAV VANG WAS A COLD-BLOODED MERCENARY. PIRACY CAME LATER WHEN HE REALIZED STEALING WAS A LOT SAFER THAN DROPPING INTO WAR ZONES.
I TOLD THE KING WE COULD TAKE BACK THE HUDSON WITHOUT HIM, BUT THE CANCER MADE HIM STUBBORN AND SCARED.
HE WANTED ELIZABETH TO ASCEND TO THE THRONE AND RULE IN A TIME PEACE AND HE DIDN'T WANT TO DIE WITHOUT RESOLVING THE CONFLICT SO HE PROMISED TO MAKE VANG A DUKE.
BUT THE QUEEN DIDN'T HONOR THAT BARGAIN. DID YOU ADVISE HER AGAINST IT?
WE MAY BE FRIENDS, BUT I'M JUST A KNIGHT, AYLA.
WHEN I TURNED DOWN THE JOB SHE GAVE IT TO VANG.
WHY'D YOU TURN IT DOWN?
POLITICS AND BOREDOM. MOST OF YOUR TIME IS SPENT SHAKING HANDS, MONITORING DEPARTMENTS AND MAKING SPEECHES WHEN SHIT GOES SOUTH.
LIKE I SAID, I'M A KNIGHT. I BELIEVE IN WHAT WE DO AND WHAT WE STAND FOR.
IF VANG IS WILLING TO MAIM AND KILL HUNDREDS OF INNOCENT PEOPLE WHAT'S HE AFTER?
ISN'T IT OBVIOUS?

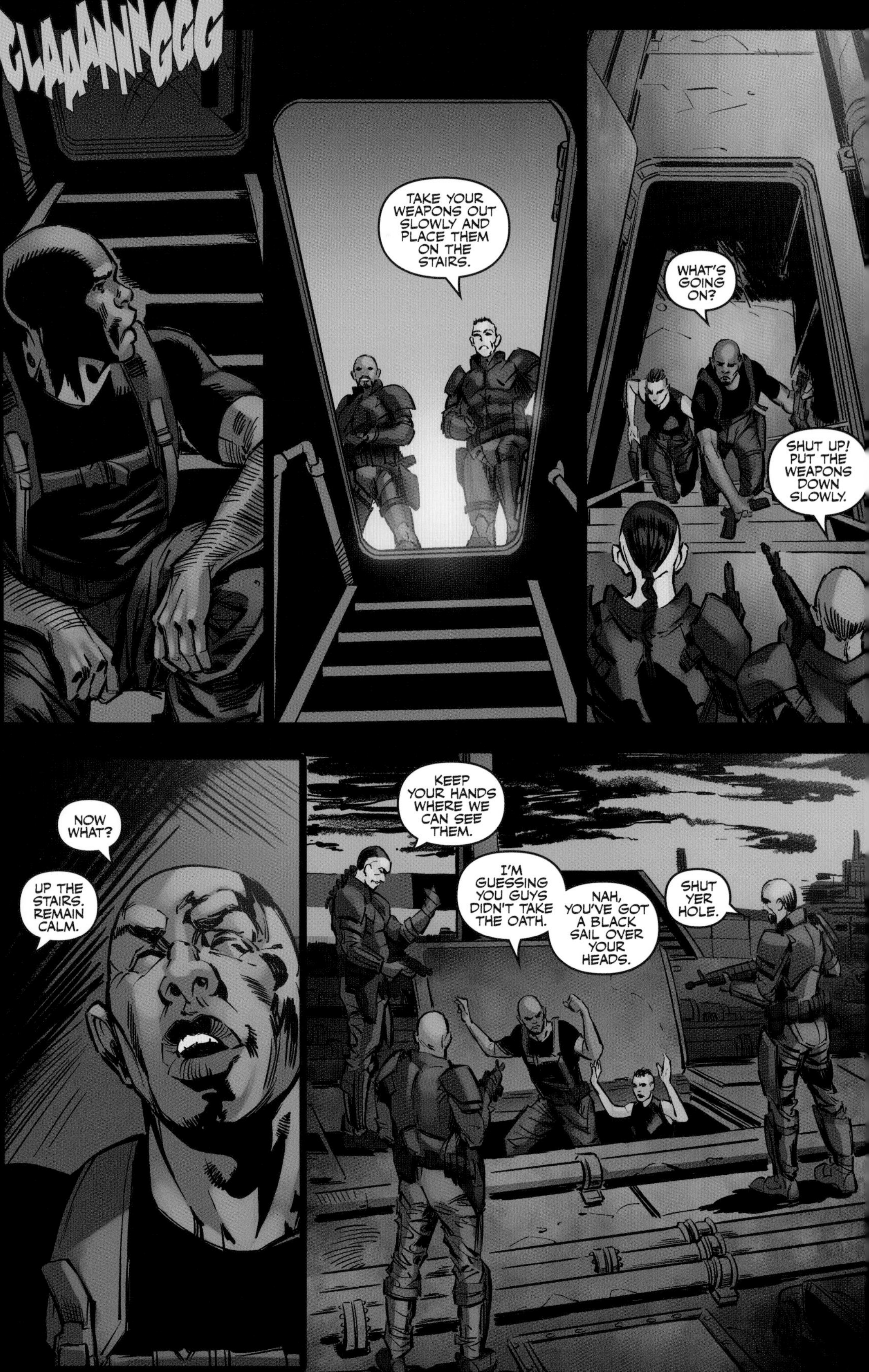
CLAAANNGGG
TAKE YOUR WEAPONS OUT SLOWLY AND PLACE THEM ON THE STAIRS.
WHAT'S GOING ON?
SHUT UP! PUT THE WEAPONS DOWN SLOWLY.
NOW WHAT?
UP THE STAIRS. REMAIN CALM.
KEEP YOUR HANDS WHERE WE CAN SEE THEM.
I'M GUESSING YOU GUYS DIDN'T TAKE THE OATH.
NAH, YOU'VE GOT A BLACK SAIL OVER YOUR HEADS.
SHUT YER HOLE.

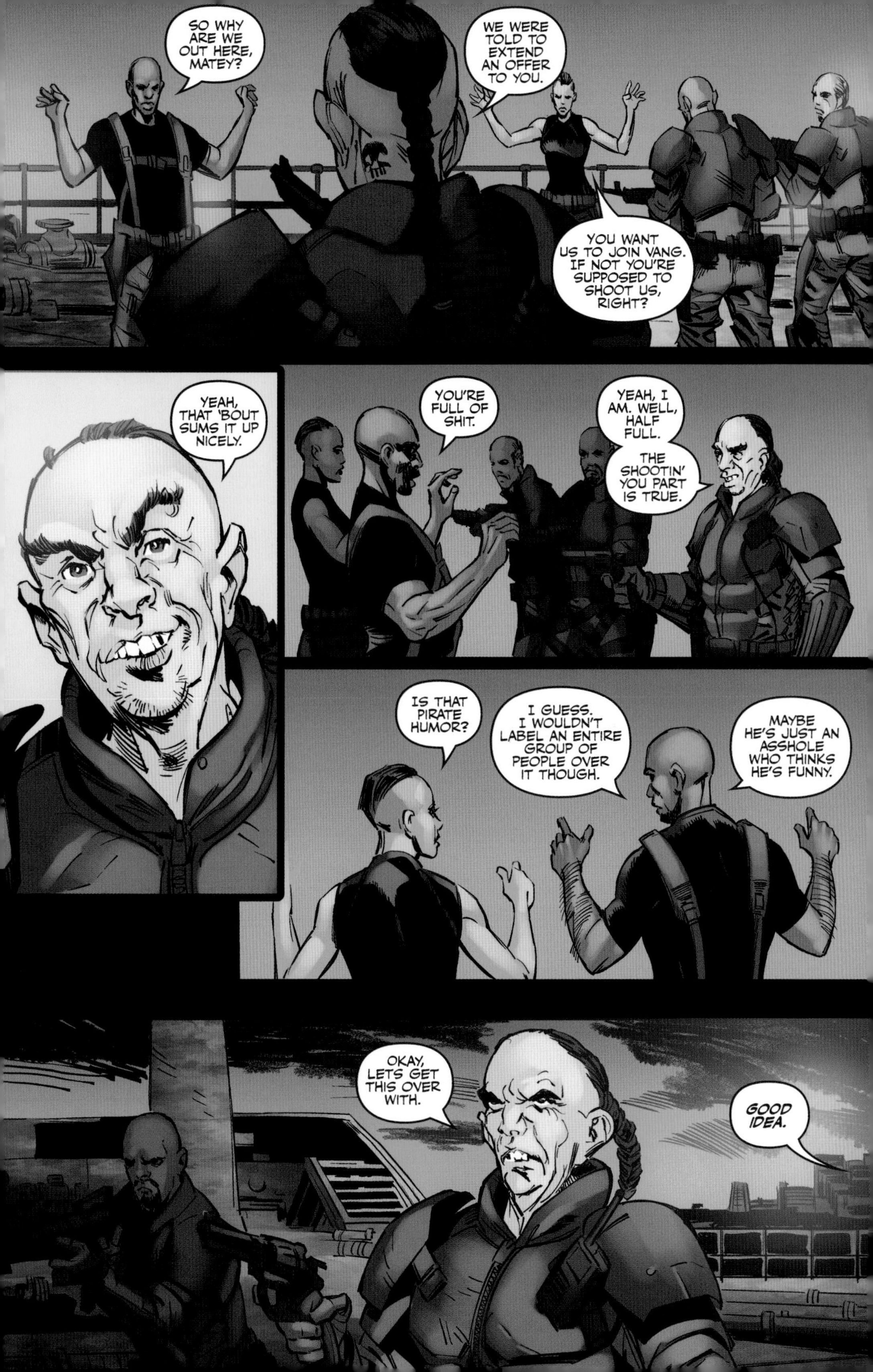
SO WHY ARE WE OUT HERE, MATEY?
WE WERE TOLD TO EXTEND AN OFFER TO YOU.
YOU WANT US TO JOIN VANG. IF NOT YOU'RE SUPPOSED TO SHOOT US, RIGHT?
YEAH, THAT 'BOUT SUMS IT UP NICELY.
YOU'RE FULL OF SHIT.
YEAH, I AM. WELL, HALF FULL.
THE SHOOTIN' YOU PART IS TRUE.
IS THAT PIRATE HUMOR?
I GUESS. I WOULDN'T LABEL AN ENTIRE GROUP OF PEOPLE OVER IT THOUGH.
MAYBE HE'S JUST AN ASSHOLE WHO THINKS HE'S FUNNY.
OKAY, LETS GET THIS OVER WITH.
GOOD IDEA.

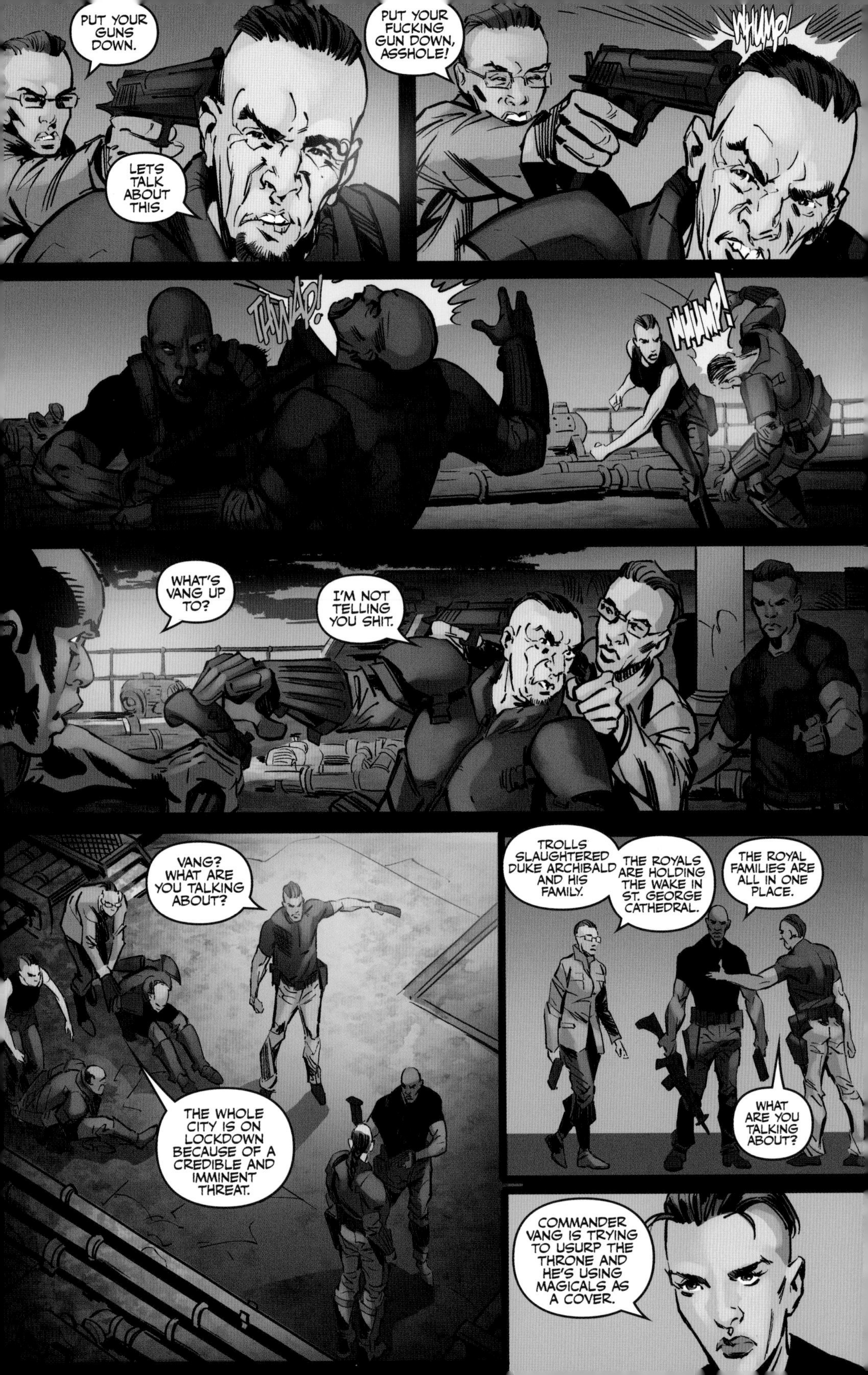
PUT YOUR GUNS DOWN.
LETS TALK ABOUT THIS.
PUT YOUR FUCKING GUN DOWN, ASSHOLE!
WHUMP!
THWAP!
WHUMP!
WHAT'S VANG UP TO?
I'M NOT TELLING YOU SHIT.
VANG? WHAT ARE YOU TALKING ABOUT?
THE WHOLE CITY IS ON LOCKDOWN BECAUSE OF A CREDIBLE AND IMMINENT THREAT.
TROLLS SLAUGHTERED DUKE ARCHIBALD AND HIS FAMILY.
THE ROYALS ARE HOLDING THE WAKE IN ST. GEORGE CATHEDRAL.
THE ROYAL FAMILIES ARE ALL IN ONE PLACE.
WHAT ARE YOU TALKING ABOUT?
COMMANDER VANG IS TRYING TO USURP THE THRONE AND HE'S USING MAGICALS AS A COVER.

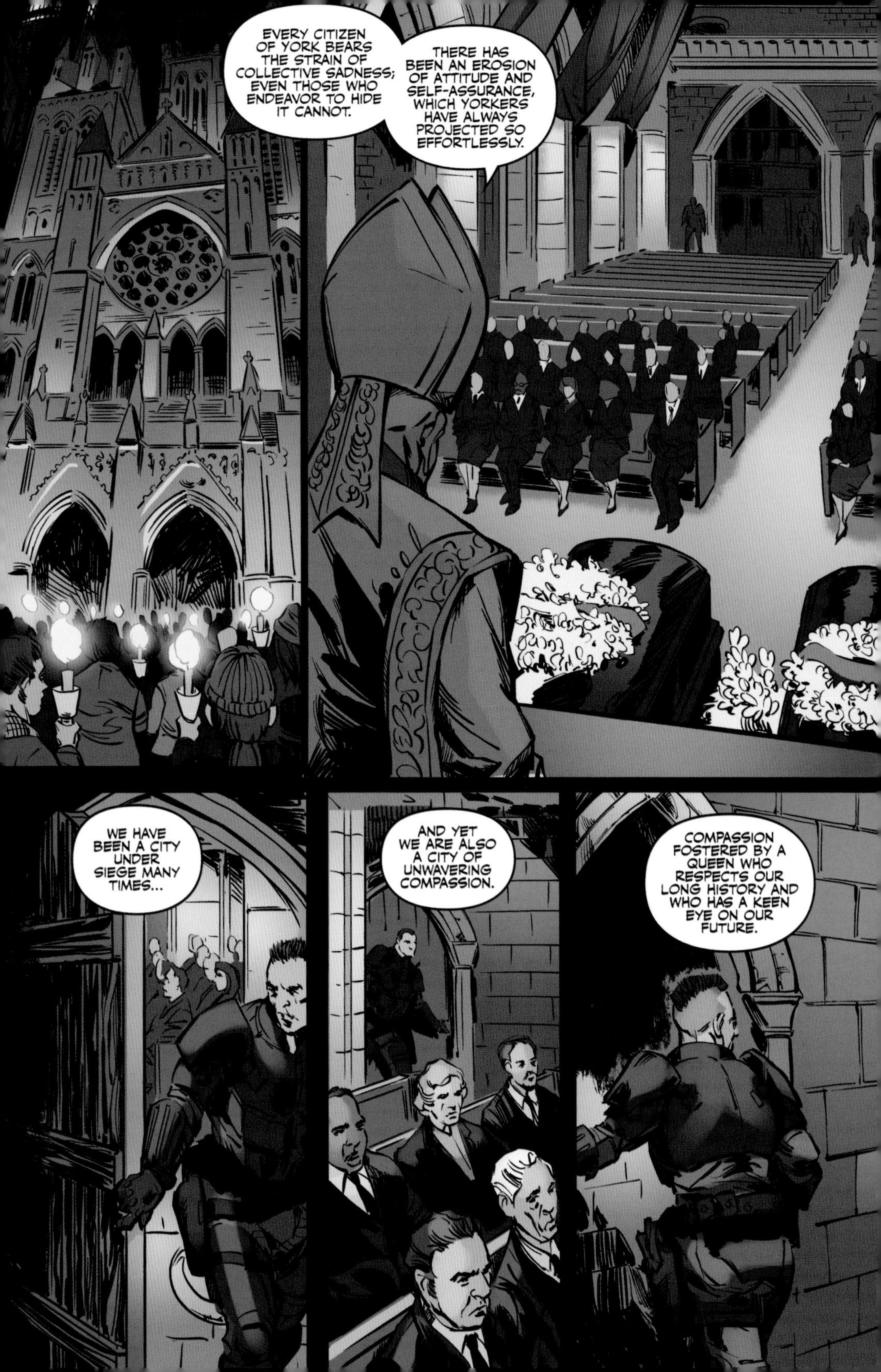
EVERY CITIZEN OF YORK BEARS THE STRAIN OF COLLECTIVE SADNESS; EVEN THOSE WHO ENDEAVOR TO HIDE IT CANNOT.
THERE HAS BEEN AN EROSION OF ATTITUDE AND SELF-ASSURANCE, WHICH YORKERS HAVE ALWAYS PROJECTED SO EFFORTLESSLY.
WE HAVE BEEN A CITY UNDER SIEGE MANY TIMES...
AND YET WE ARE ALSO A CITY OF UNWAVERING COMPASSION.
COMPASSION FOSTERED BY A QUEEN WHO RESPECTS OUR LONG HISTORY AND WHO HAS A KEEN EYE ON OUR FUTURE.

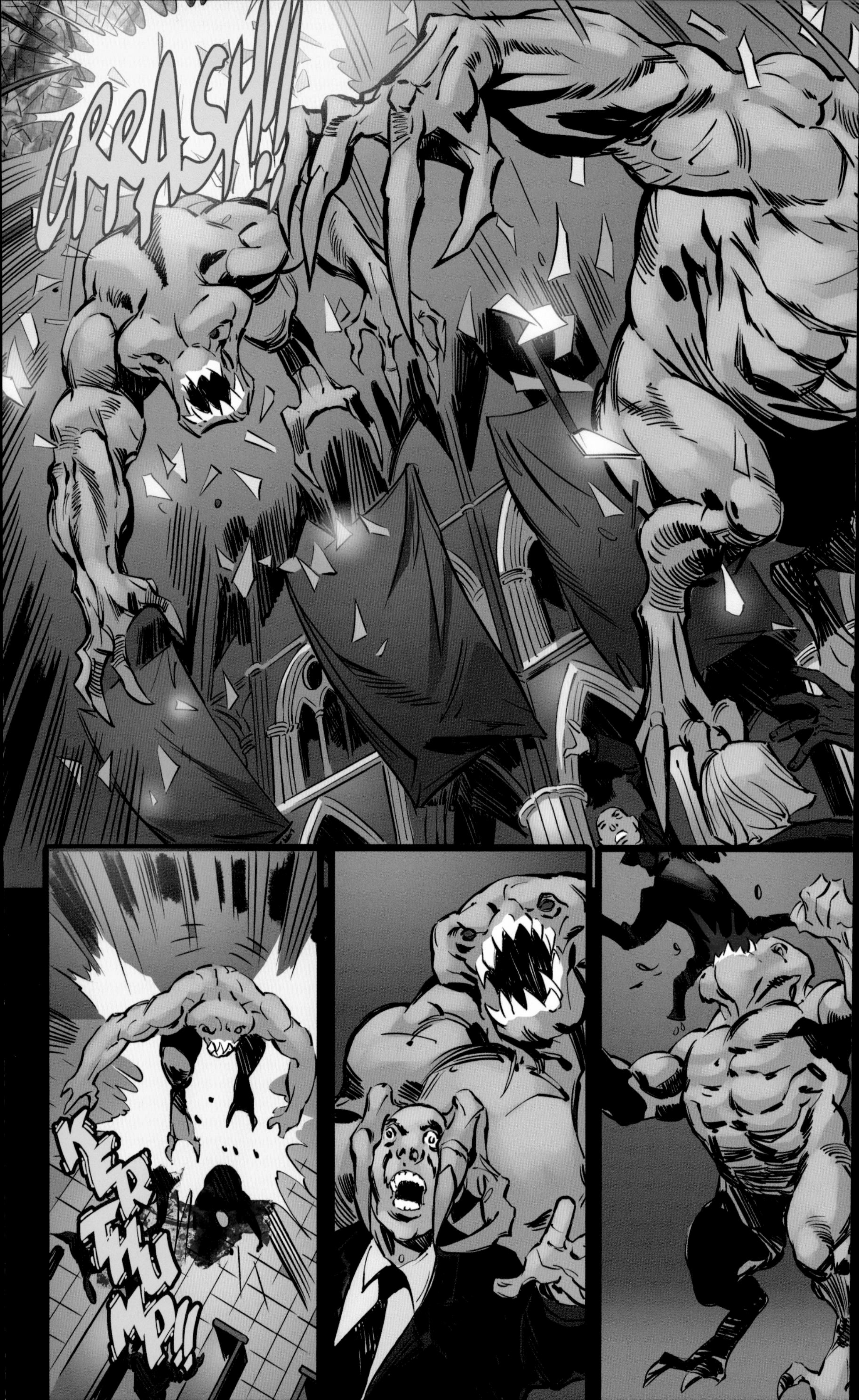
CRASH!!
KERTHUMP!!

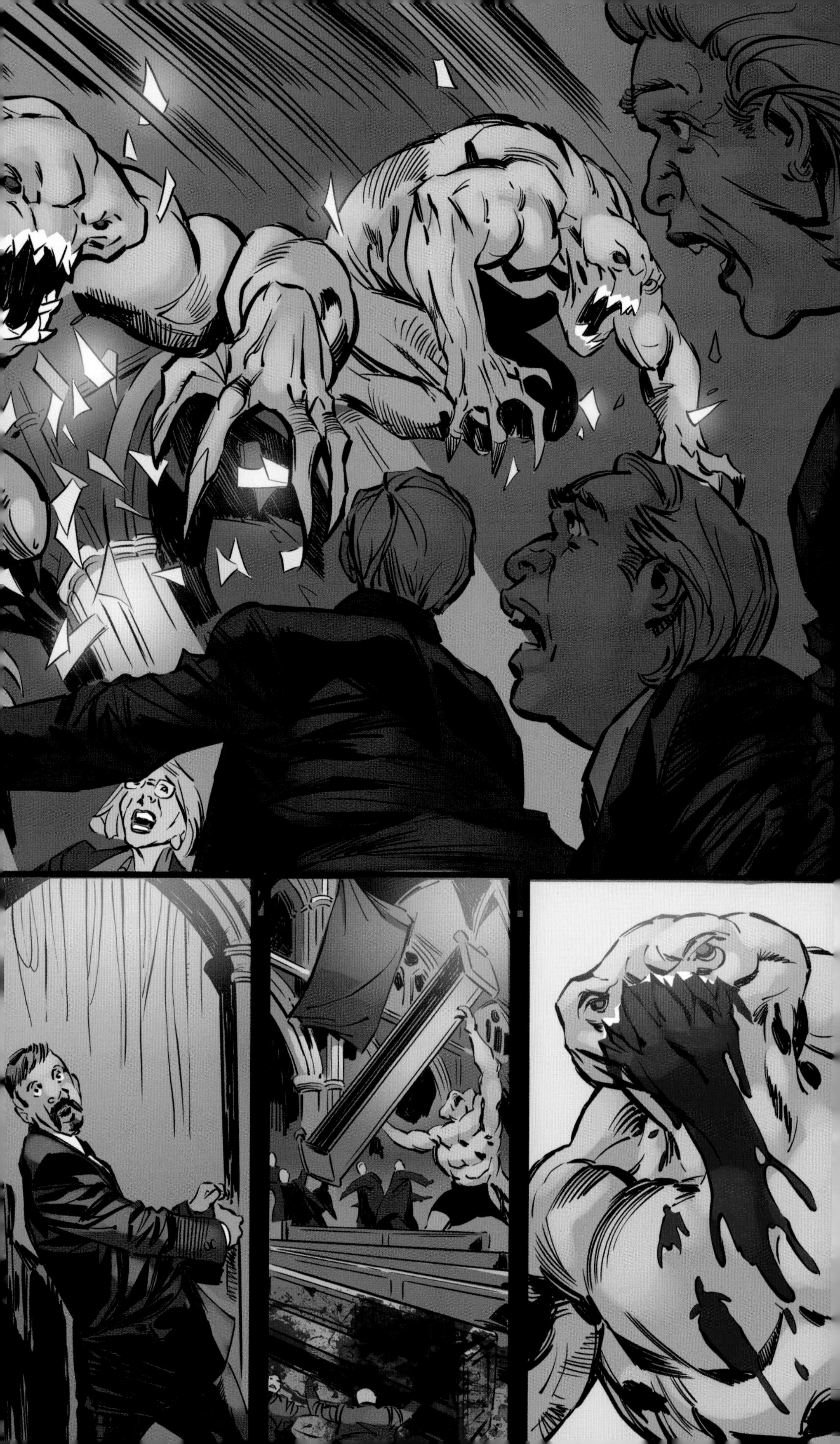

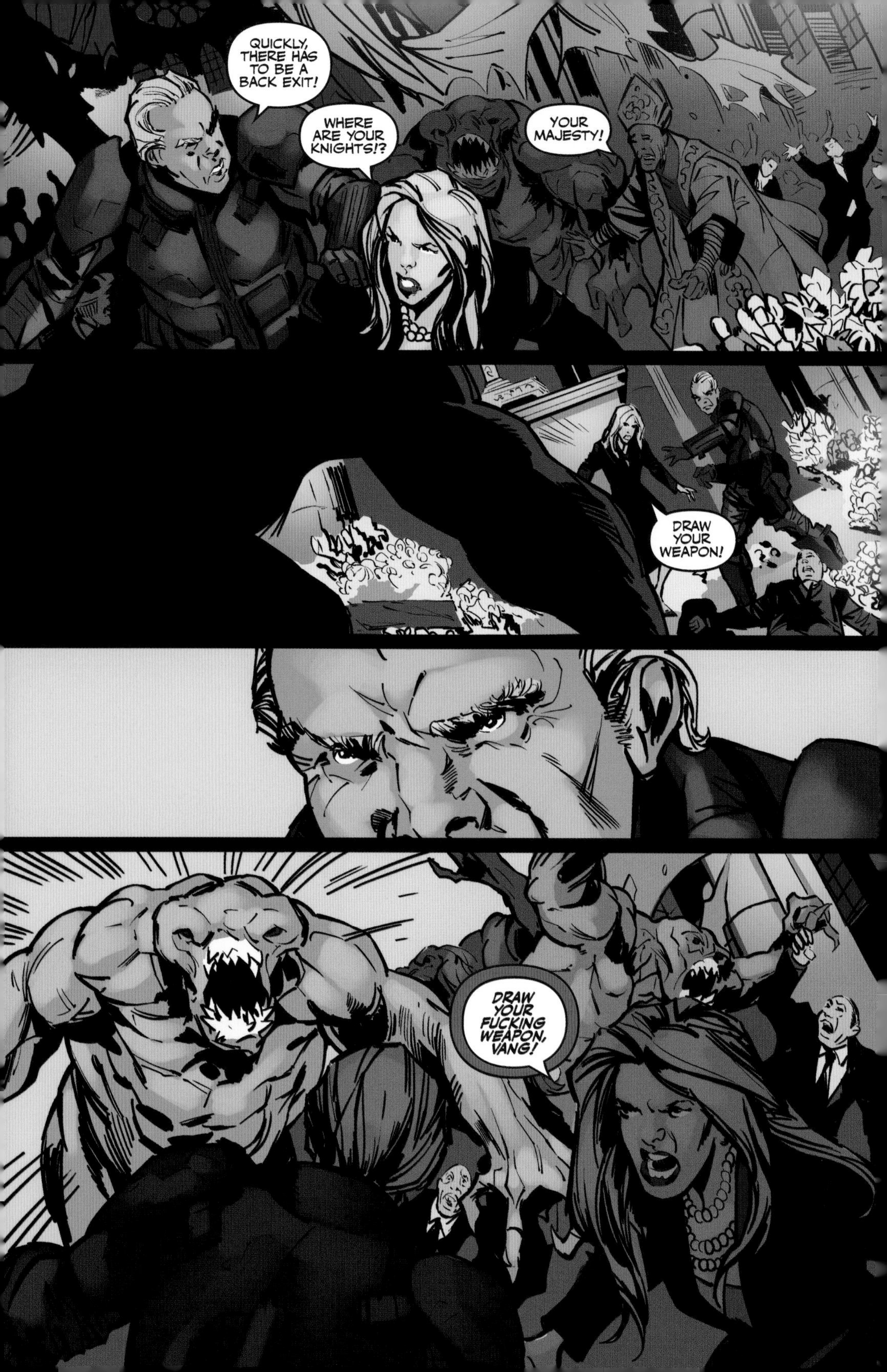
QUICKLY, THERE HAS TO BE A BACK EXIT!
WHERE ARE YOUR KNIGHTS!?
YOUR MAJESTY!
DRAW YOUR WEAPON!
DRAW YOUR FUCKING WEAPON, VANG!

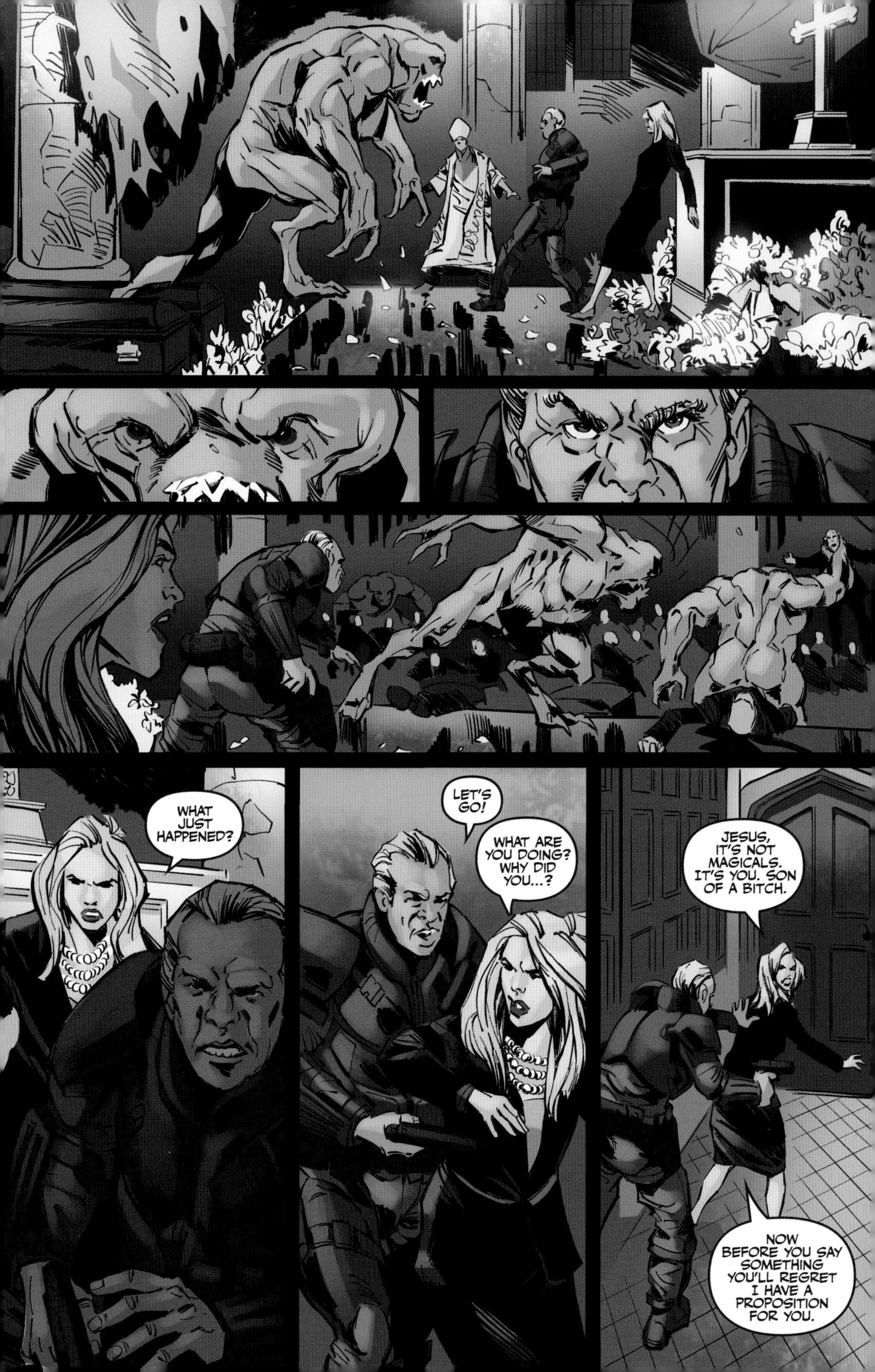
WHAT JUST HAPPENED?
LET'S GO!
WHAT ARE YOU DOING? WHY DID YOU...?
JESUS, IT'S NOT MAGICALS. IT'S YOU. SON OF A BITCH.
NOW BEFORE YOU SAY SOMETHING YOU'LL REGRET I HAVE A PROPOSITION FOR YOU.

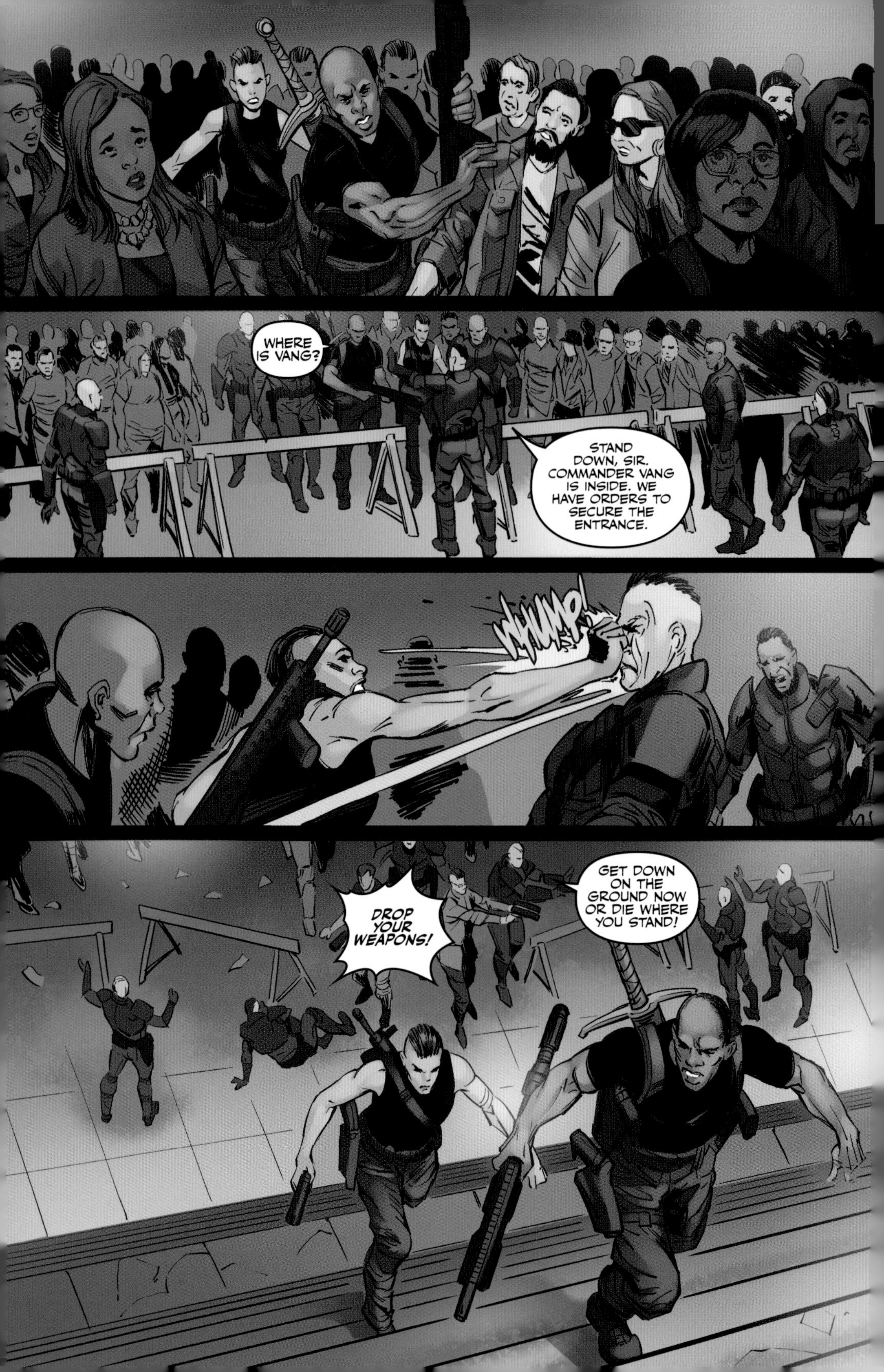
WHERE IS VANG?
STAND DOWN, SIR. COMMANDER VANG IS INSIDE. WE HAVE ORDERS TO SECURE THE ENTRANCE.
WHUMP!
DROP YOUR WEAPONS!
GET DOWN ON THE GROUND NOW OR DIE WHERE YOU STAND!

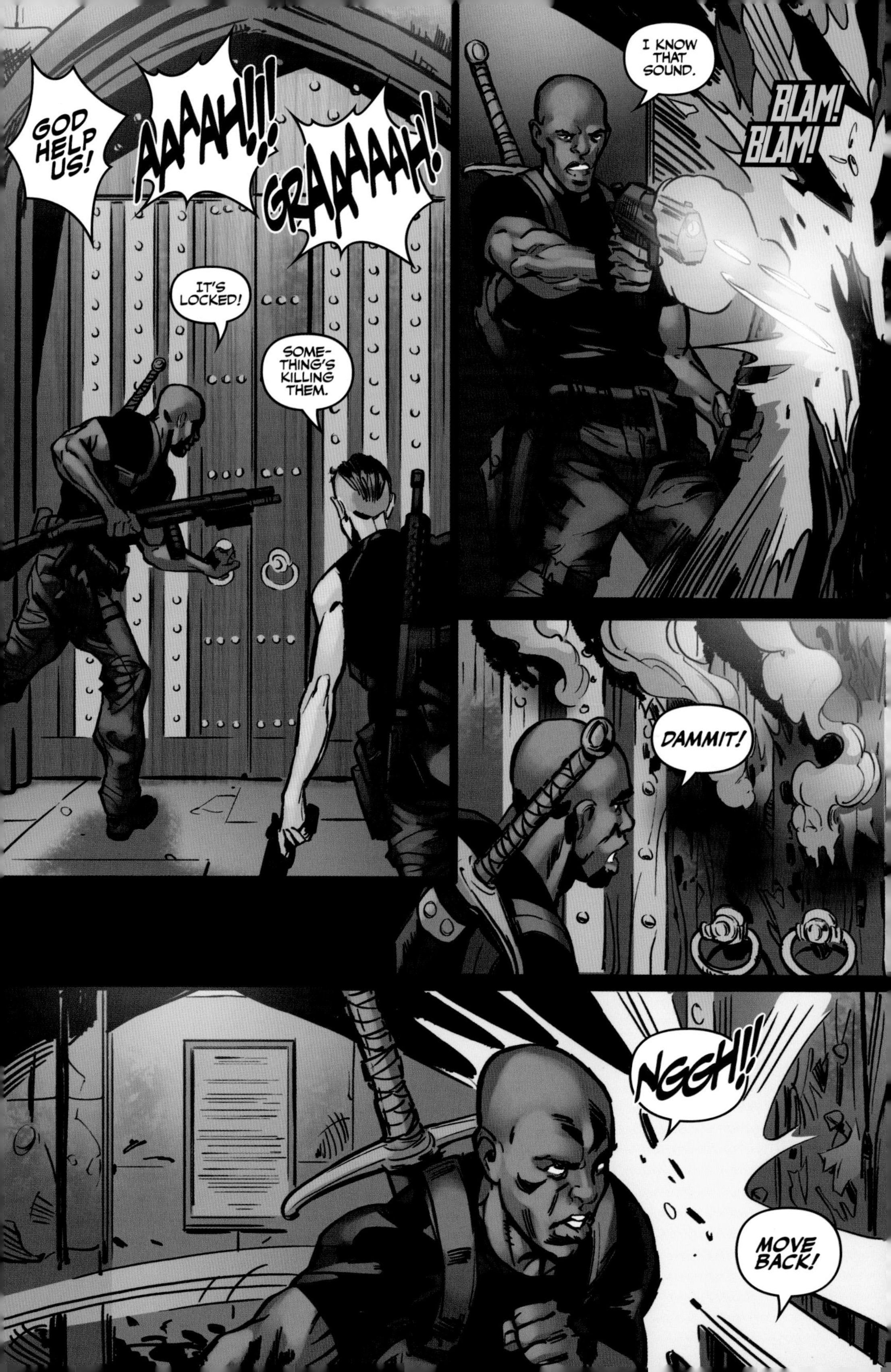
GOD HELP US!
AAAAH!!!
GRAAAAAH!
IT'S LOCKED!
SOME-THING'S KILLING THEM.
I KNOW THAT SOUND.
BLAM! BLAM!
DAMMIT!
NGGH!!
MOVE BACK!

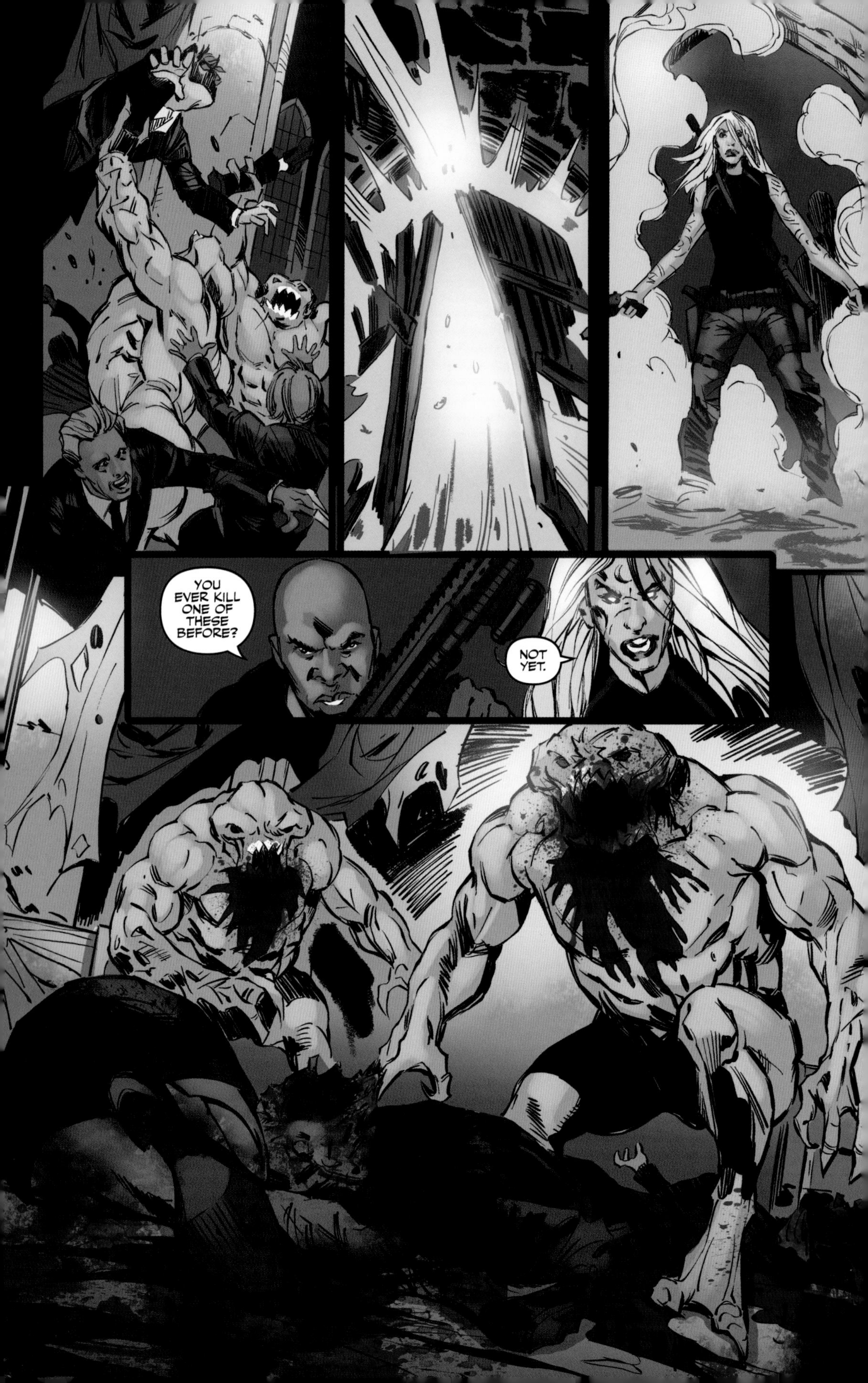
YOU EVER KILL ONE OF THESE BEFORE?
NOT YET.

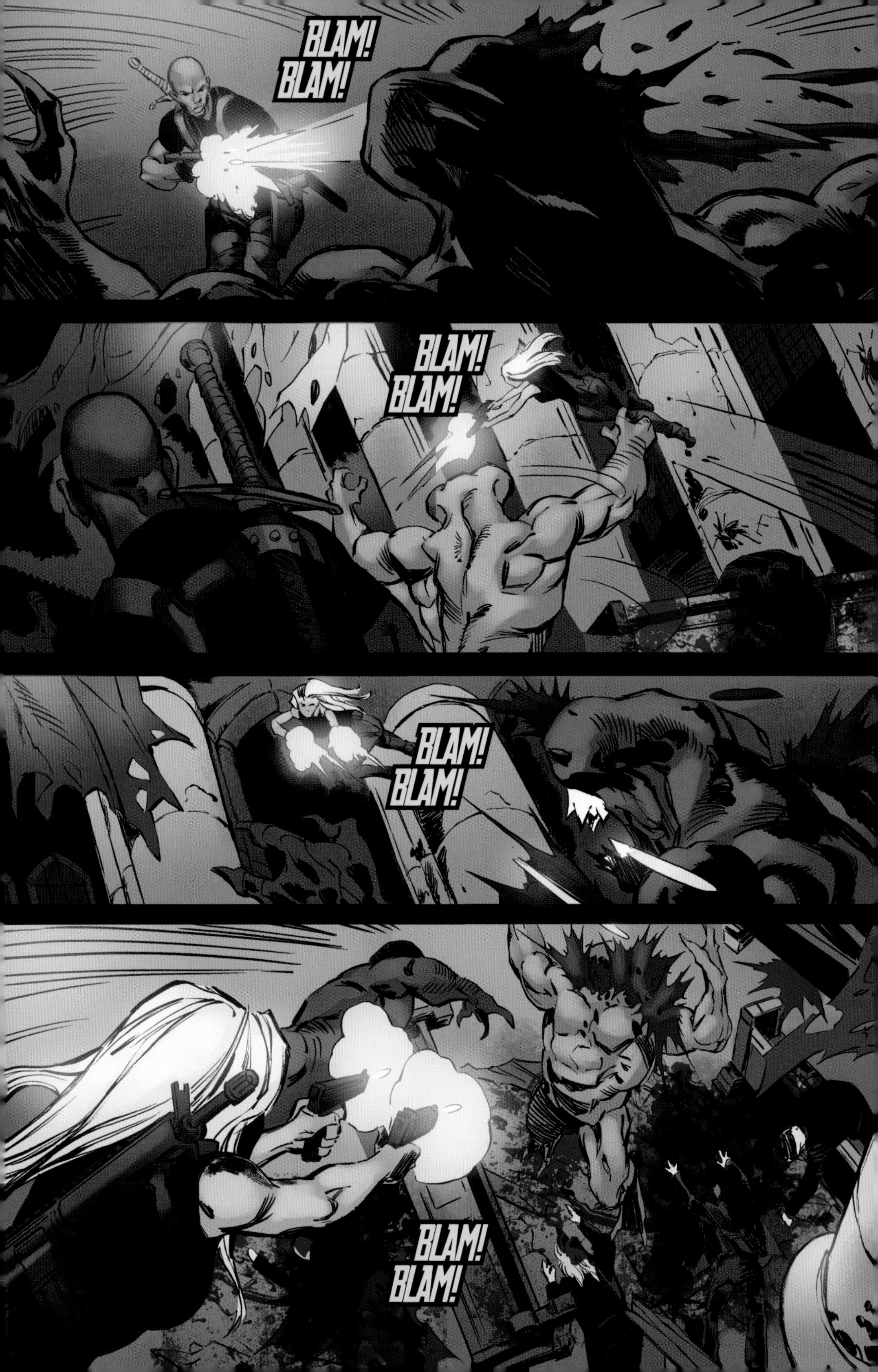
BLAM! BLAM!
BLAM! BLAM!
BLAM! BLAM!
BLAM! BLAM!

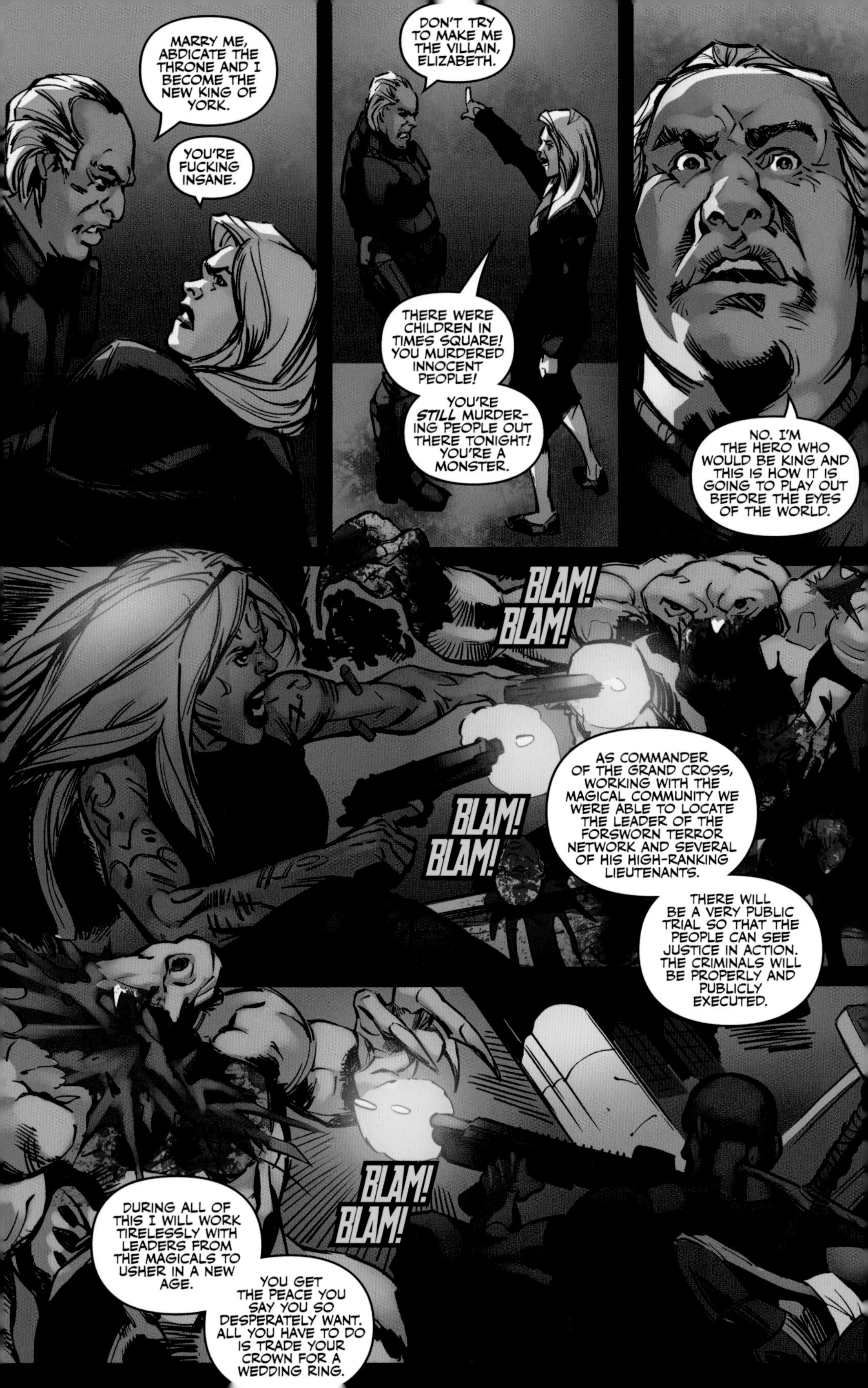
MARRY ME, ABDICATE THE THRONE AND I BECOME THE NEW KING OF YORK.
YOU'RE FUCKING INSANE.
DON'T TRY TO MAKE ME THE VILLAIN, ELIZABETH.
THERE WERE CHILDREN IN TIMES SQUARE! YOU MURDERED INNOCENT PEOPLE!
YOU'RE STILL MURDERING PEOPLE OUT THERE TONIGHT! YOU'RE A MONSTER.
NO. I'M THE HERO WHO WOULD BE KING AND THIS IS HOW IT IS GOING TO PLAY OUT BEFORE THE EYES OF THE WORLD.
BLAM! BLAM!
BLAM! BLAM!
AS COMMANDER OF THE GRAND CROSS, WORKING WITH THE MAGICAL COMMUNITY WE WERE ABLE TO LOCATE THE LEADER OF THE FORSWORN TERROR NETWORK AND SEVERAL OF HIS HIGH-RANKING LIEUTENANTS.
THERE WILL BE A VERY PUBLIC TRIAL SO THAT THE PEOPLE CAN SEE JUSTICE IN ACTION. THE CRIMINALS WILL BE PROPERLY AND PUBLICLY EXECUTED.
BLAM! BLAM!
DURING ALL OF THIS I WILL WORK TIRELESSLY WITH LEADERS FROM THE MAGICALS TO USHER IN A NEW AGE.
YOU GET THE PEACE YOU SAY YOU SO DESPERATELY WANT. ALL YOU HAVE TO DO IS TRADE YOUR CROWN FOR A WEDDING RING.

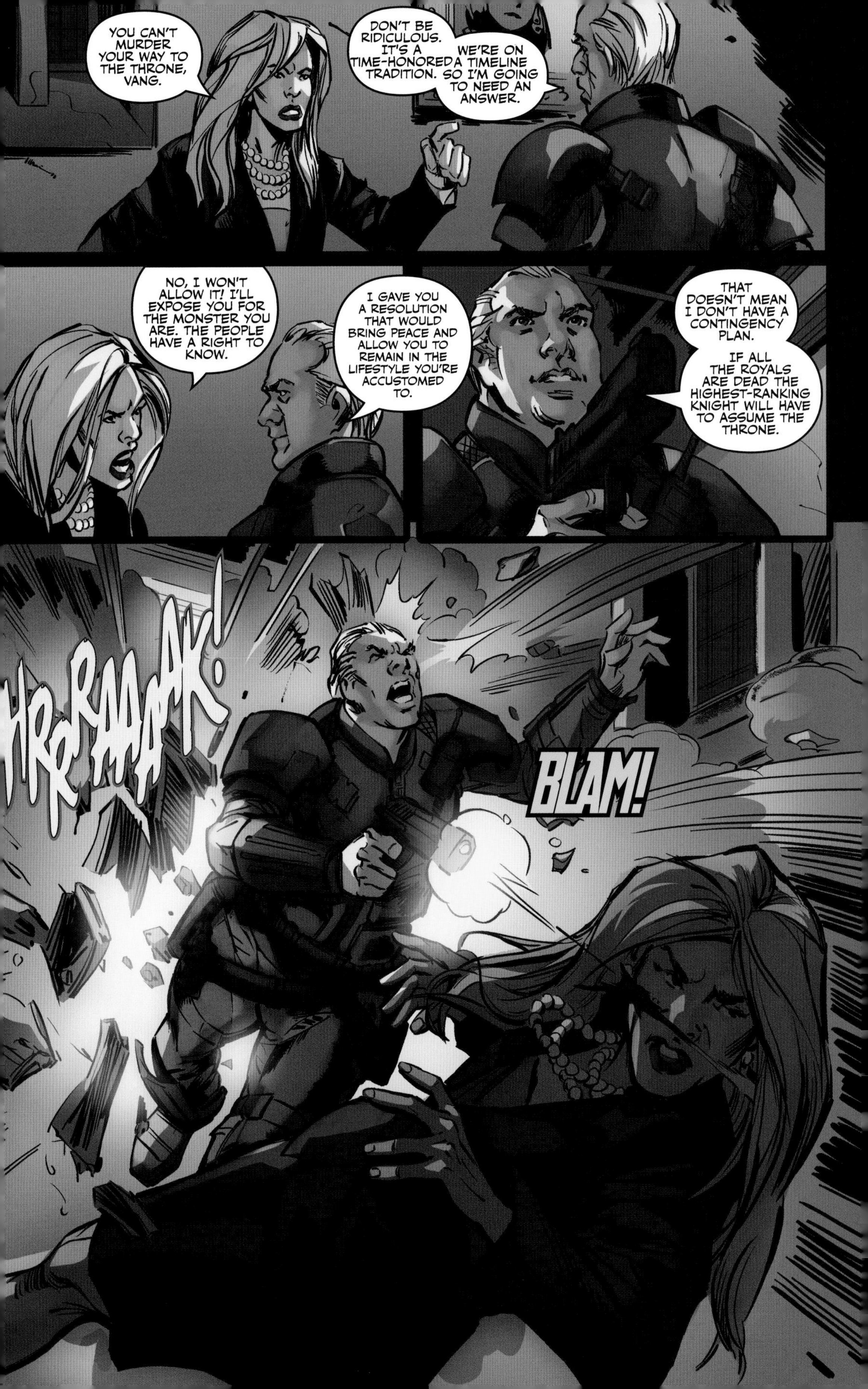
YOU CAN'T MURDER YOUR WAY TO THE THRONE, VANG.
DON'T BE RIDICULOUS. IT'S A TIME-HONORED TRADITION.
WE'RE ON A TIMELINE SO I'M GOING TO NEED AN ANSWER.
NO, I WON'T ALLOW IT! I'LL EXPOSE YOU FOR THE MONSTER YOU ARE. THE PEOPLE HAVE A RIGHT TO KNOW.
I GAVE YOU A RESOLUTION THAT WOULD BRING PEACE AND ALLOW YOU TO REMAIN IN THE LIFESTYLE YOU'RE ACCUSTOMED TO.
THAT DOESN'T MEAN I DON'T HAVE A CONTINGENCY PLAN.
IF ALL THE ROYALS ARE DEAD THE HIGHEST-RANKING KNIGHT WILL HAVE TO ASSUME THE THRONE.
HRRRAAAAK!
BLAM!

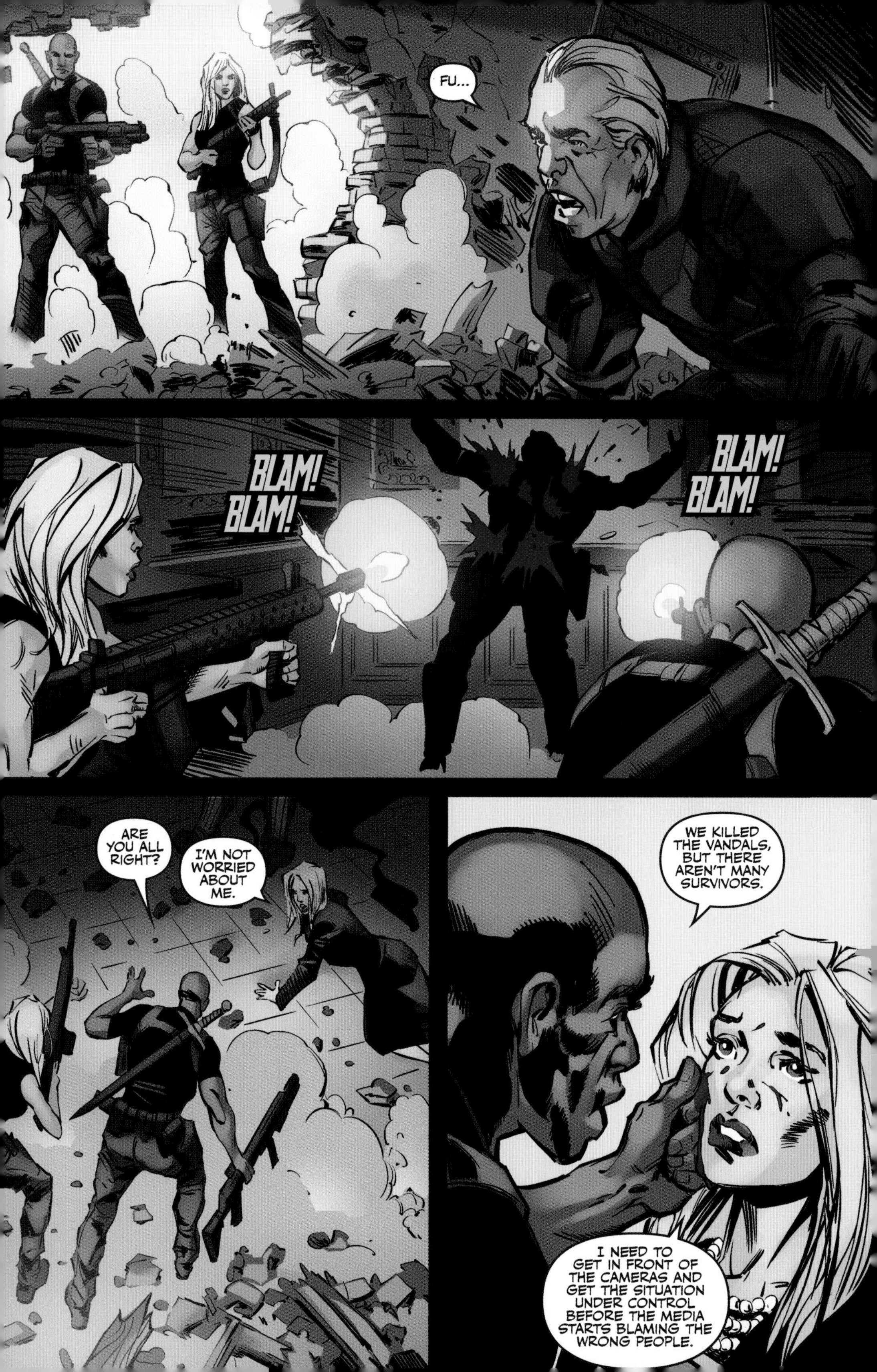
FU...
BLAM! BLAM!
BLAM! BLAM!
ARE YOU ALL RIGHT?
I'M NOT WORRIED ABOUT ME.
WE KILLED THE VANDALS, BUT THERE AREN'T MANY SURVIVORS.
I NEED TO GET IN FRONT OF THE CAMERAS AND GET THE SITUATION UNDER CONTROL BEFORE THE MEDIA STARTS BLAMING THE WRONG PEOPLE.

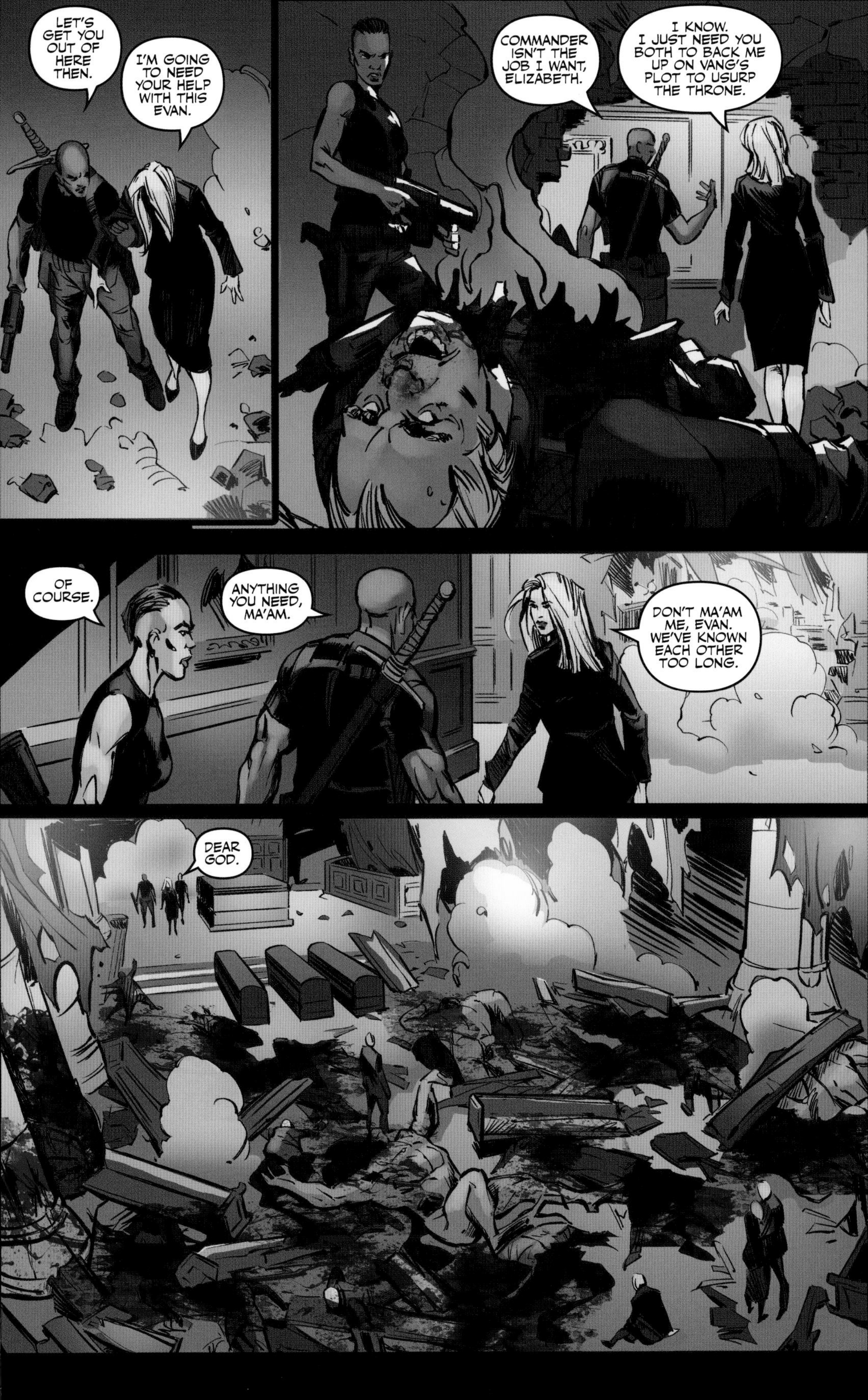
LET'S GET YOU OUT OF HERE THEN.
I'M GOING TO NEED YOUR HELP WITH THIS EVAN.
COMMANDER ISN'T THE JOB I WANT, ELIZABETH.
I KNOW. I JUST NEED YOU BOTH TO BACK ME UP ON VANG'S PLOT TO USURP THE THRONE.
OF COURSE.
ANYTHING YOU NEED, MA'AM.
DON'T MA'AM ME, EVAN. WE'VE KNOWN EACH OTHER TOO LONG.
DEAR GOD.

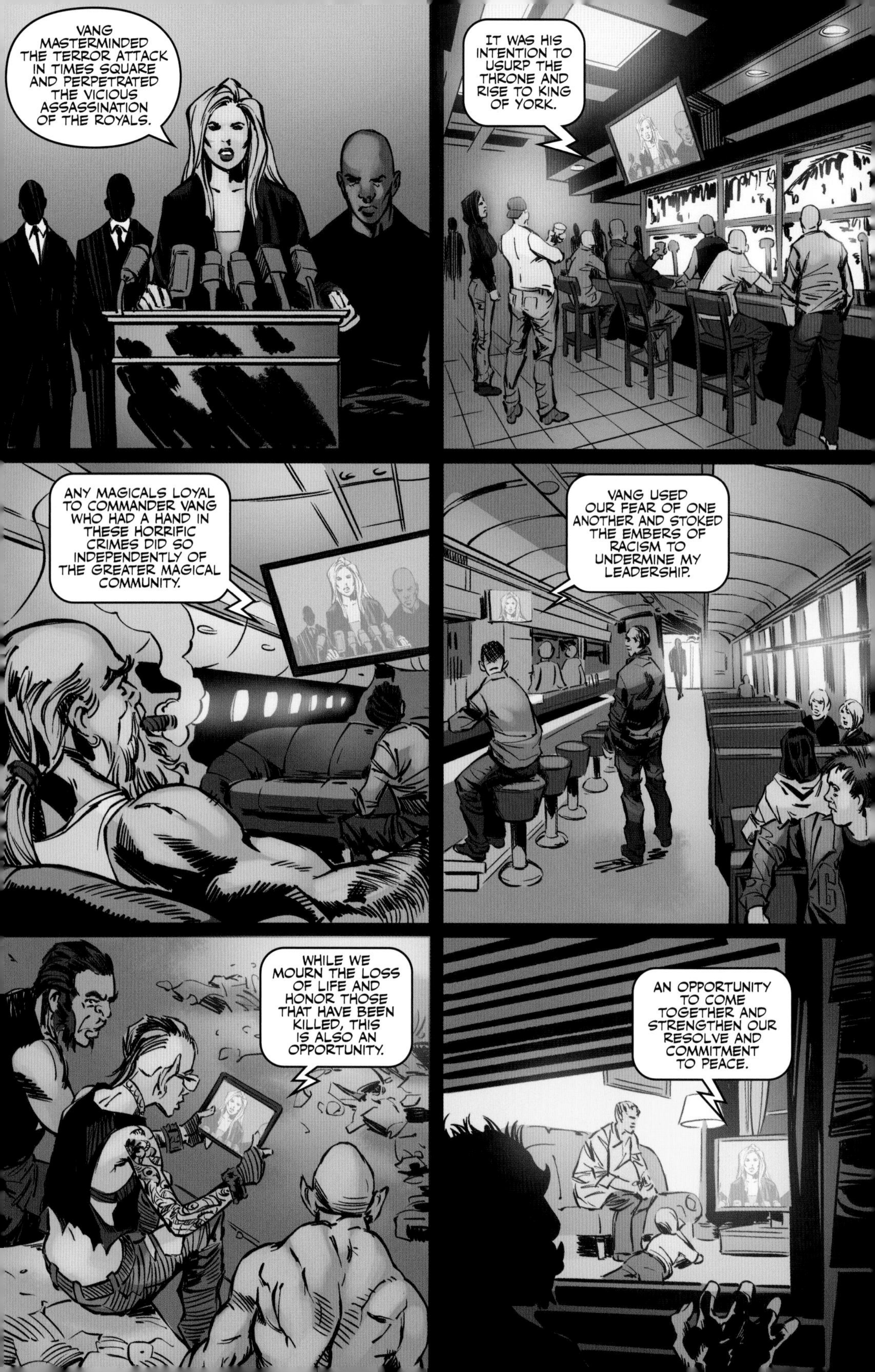
VANG MASTERMINDED THE TERROR ATTACK IN TIMES SQUARE AND PERPETRATED THE VICIOUS ASSASSINATION OF THE ROYALS.
IT WAS HIS INTENTION TO USURP THE THRONE AND RISE TO KING OF YORK.
ANY MAGICALS LOYAL TO COMMANDER VANG WHO HAD A HAND IN THESE HORRIFIC CRIMES DID SO INDEPENDENTLY OF THE GREATER MAGICAL COMMUNITY.
VANG USED OUR FEAR OF ONE ANOTHER AND STOKED THE EMBERS OF RACISM TO UNDERMINE MY LEADERSHIP.
WHILE WE MOURN THE LOSS OF LIFE AND HONOR THOSE THAT HAVE BEEN KILLED, THIS IS ALSO AN OPPORTUNITY.
AN OPPORTUNITY TO COME TOGETHER AND STRENGTHEN OUR RESOLVE AND COMMITMENT TO PEACE.

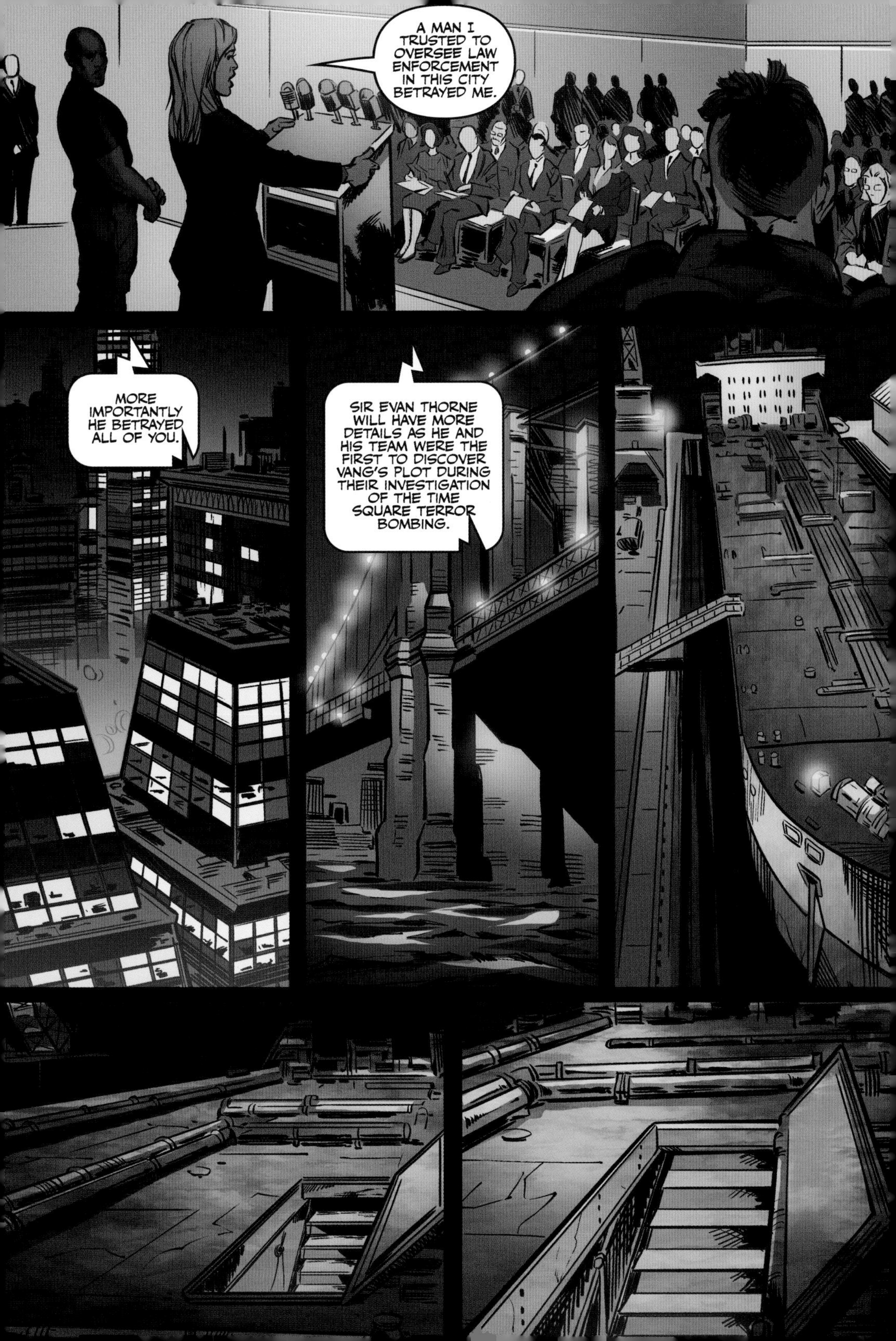
A MAN I TRUSTED TO OVERSEE LAW ENFORCEMENT IN THIS CITY BETRAYED ME.
MORE IMPORTANTLY HE BETRAYED ALL OF YOU.
SIR EVAN THORNE WILL HAVE MORE DETAILS AS HE AND HIS TEAM WERE THE FIRST TO DISCOVER VANG'S PLOT DURING THEIR INVESTIGATION OF THE TIME SQUARE TERROR BOMBING.

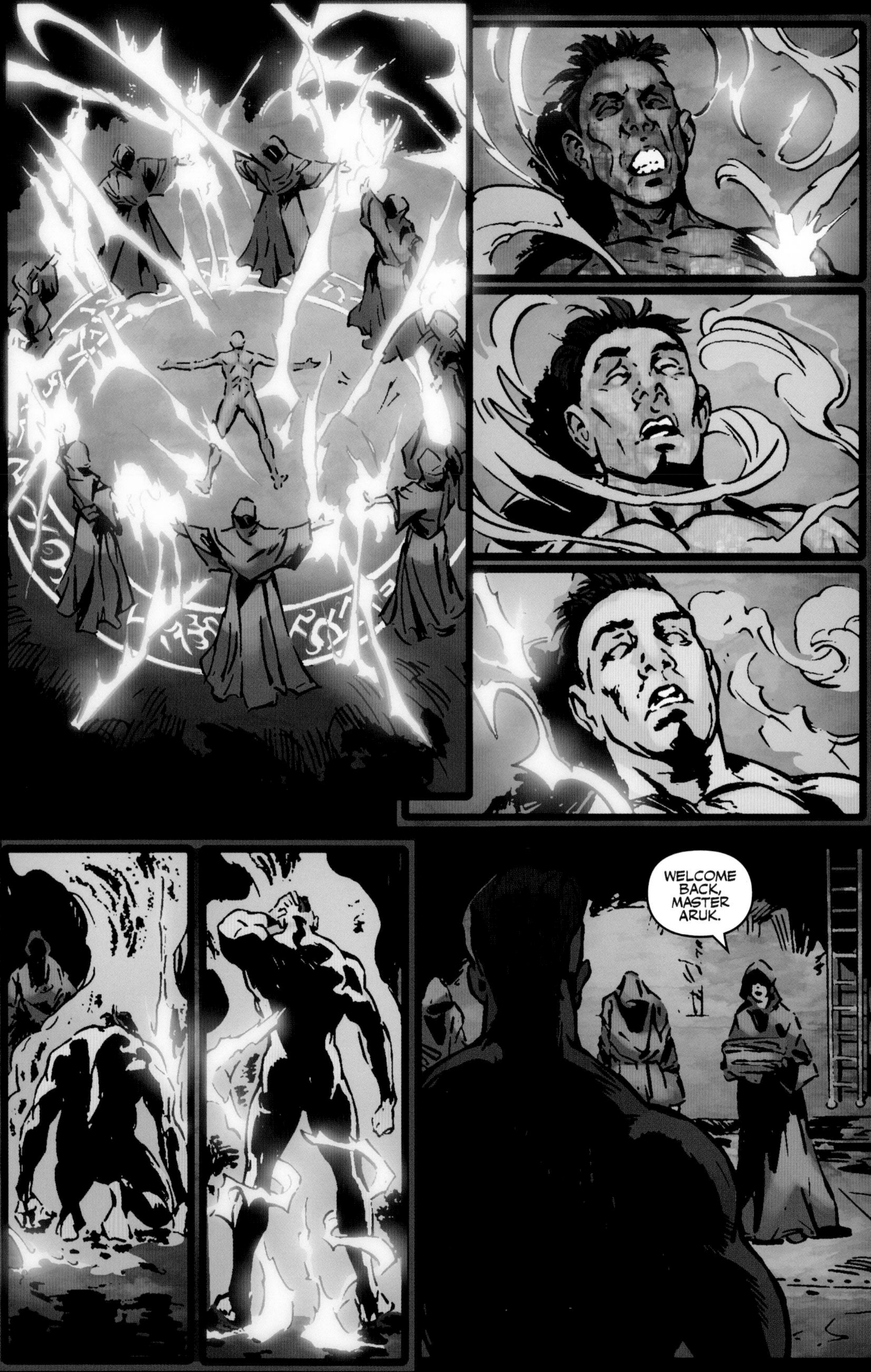
WELCOME BACK, MASTER ARUK.

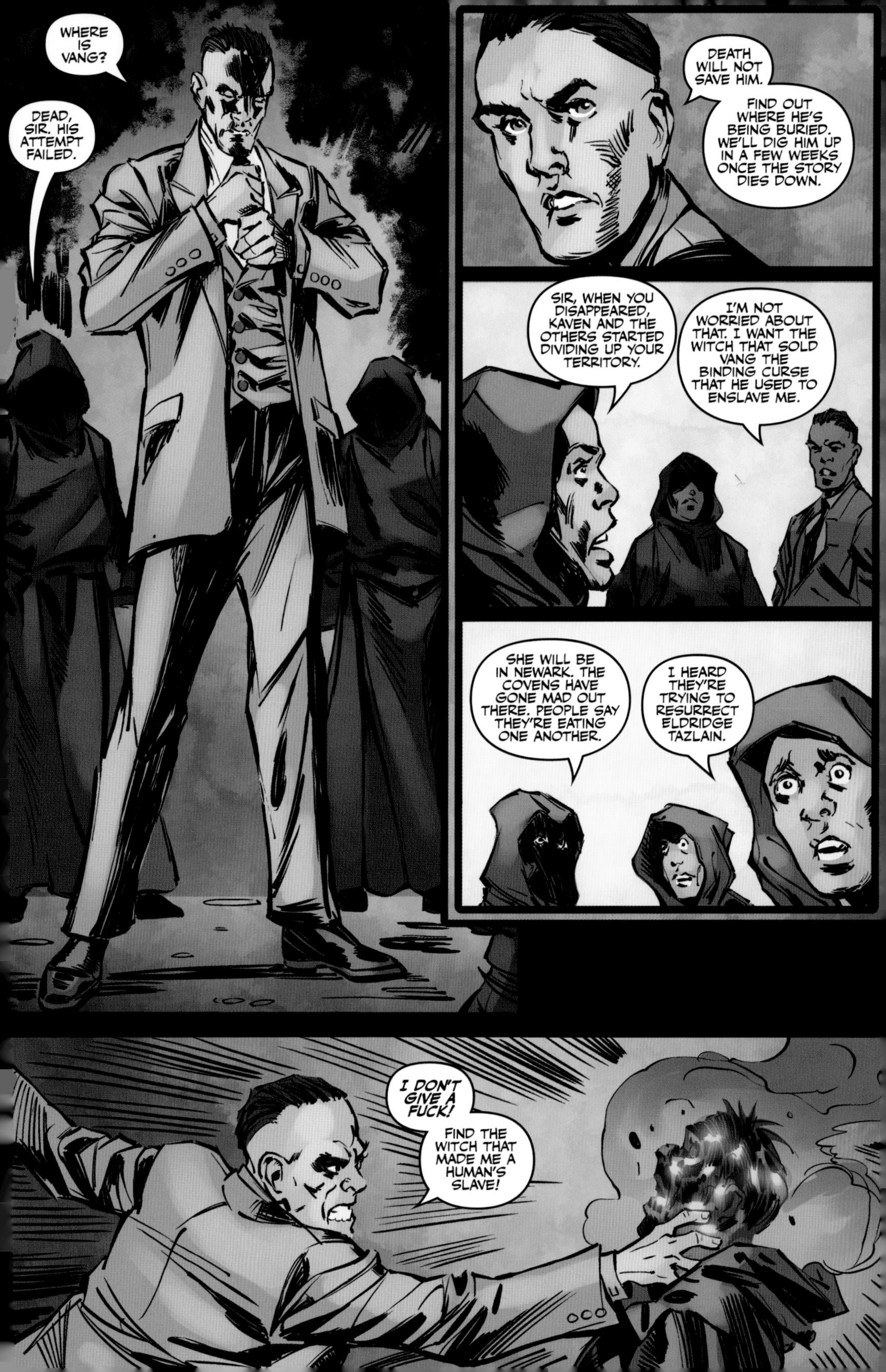
WHERE IS VANG?
DEAD, SIR. HIS ATTEMPT FAILED.
DEATH WILL NOT SAVE HIM.
FIND OUT WHERE HE'S BEING BURIED. WE'LL DIG HIM UP IN A FEW WEEKS ONCE THE STORY DIES DOWN.
SIR, WHEN YOU DISAPPEARED, KAVEN AND THE OTHERS STARTED DIVIDING UP YOUR TERRITORY.
I'M NOT WORRIED ABOUT THAT. I WANT THE WITCH THAT SOLD VANG THE BINDING CURSE THAT HE USED TO ENSLAVE ME.
SHE WILL BE IN NEWARK. THE COVENS HAVE GONE MAD OUT THERE. PEOPLE SAY THEY'RE EATING ONE ANOTHER.
I HEARD THEY'RE TRYING TO RESURRECT ELDRIDGE TAZLAIN.
I DON'T GIVE A FUCK!
FIND THE WITCH THAT MADE ME A HUMAN'S SLAVE!

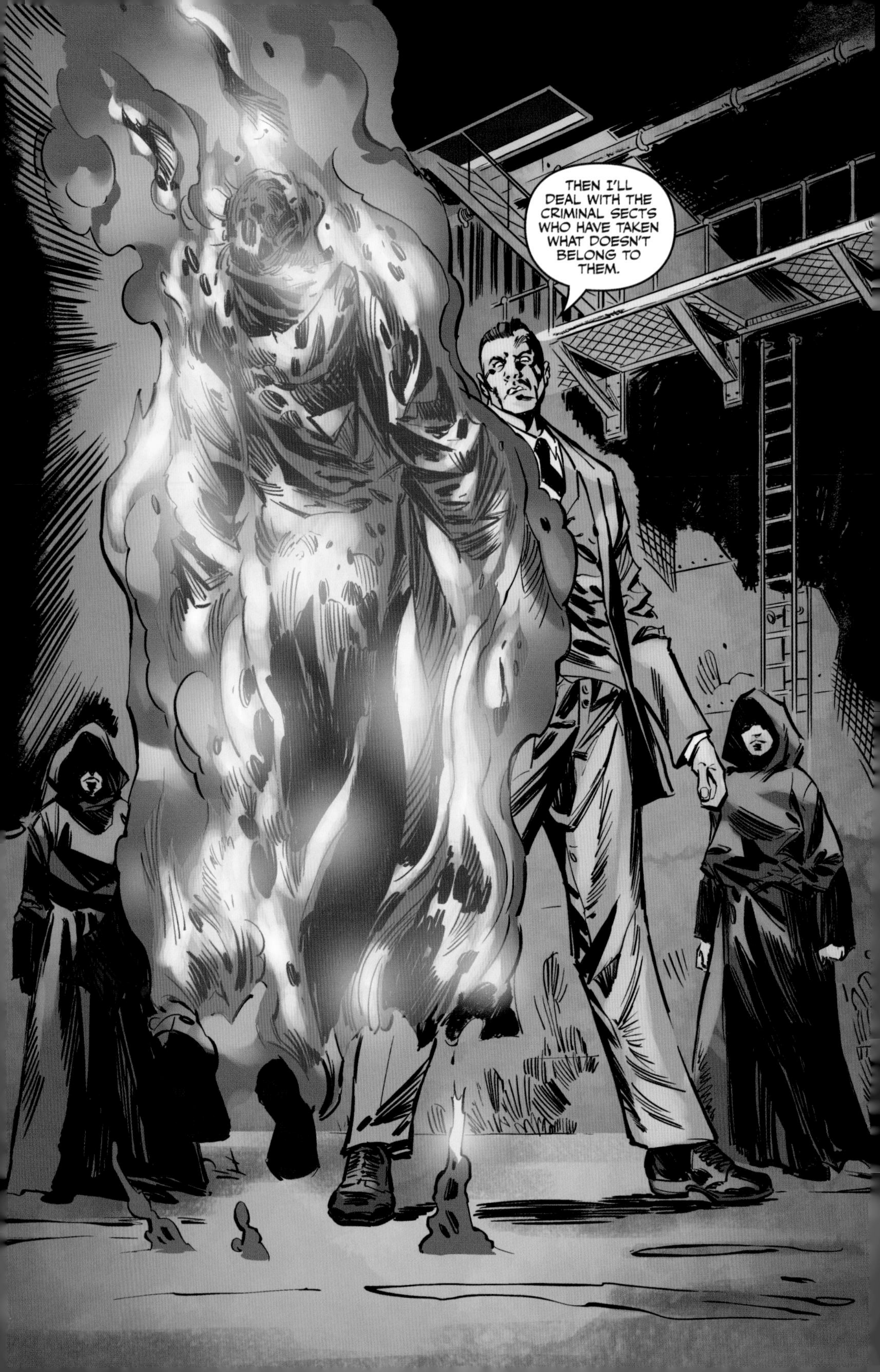
THEN I'LL DEAL WITH THE CRIMINAL SECTS WHO HAVE TAKEN WHAT DOESN'T BELONG TO THEM.

JIMMY PALMIOTTI

is a multi-award-winning writer and comic artist and the co-founder of Event Comics, Black Bull Media, Marvel Knights, and most recently, Paperfilms.

JUSTIN GRAY

has collaborated with Jimmy Palmiotti on works such as the TV series *Painkiller Jane*, *Power Girl* and *Jonah Hex* for DC Comics, *Back to Brooklyn* for Image Comics, and *Spartacus* for Devil's Due.